HANNAH BAYLES TALLENTIRE FAMILY TREE

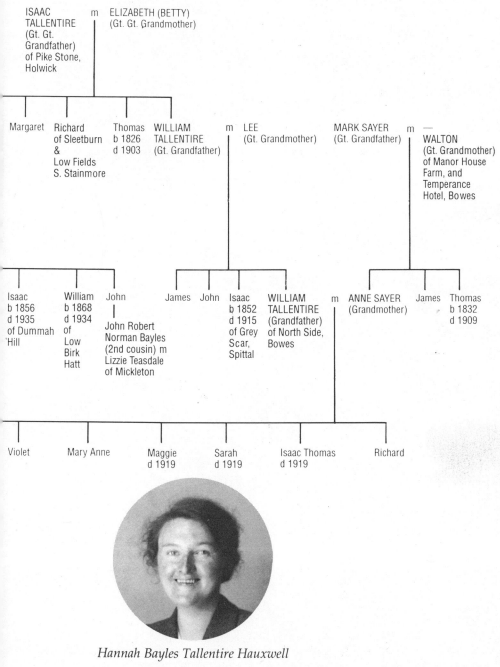

ISAAC TALLENTIRE (Gt. Gt. Grandfather) of Pike Stone, Holwick **m** ELIZABETH (BETTY) (Gt. Gt. Grandmother)

Margaret

Richard of Sleetburn & Low Fields S. Stainmore

Thomas b 1826 d 1903

WILLIAM TALLENTIRE (Gt. Grandfather) **m** LEE (Gt. Grandmother)

MARK SAYER (Gt. Grandfather) **m** — WALTON (Gt. Grandmother) of Manor House Farm, and Temperance Hotel, Bowes

Isaac b 1856 d 1935 of Dummah Hill

William b 1868 d 1934 of Low Birk Hatt

John
|
John Robert Norman Bayles (2nd cousin) m Lizzie Teasdale of Mickleton

James   John

Isaac b 1852 d 1915 of Grey Scar, Spittal

WILLIAM TALLENTIRE (Grandfather) of North Side, Bowes **m** ANNE SAYER (Grandmother)

James

Thomas b 1832 d 1909

Violet

Mary Anne

Maggie d 1919

Sarah d 1919

Isaac Thomas d 1919

Richard

Hannah Bayles Tallentire Hauxwell

Hannah

Hannah

The Complete Story

Hannah Hauxwell
with Barry Cockcroft

also by Barry Cockcroft
Hannah in Yorkshire
The Ways of a Yorkshire Dale
The Dale that Died
Princes of the Plough
A Romany Summer
A Celebration of Yorkshire
Seasons of My Life
Daughter of the Dales

This edition copyright © Tracestar Ltd 1991

The right of Barry Cockcroft to be identified as the author of this work has been asserted by him in accordance with the Copyright, Designs and Patents Act, 1988

First published by Random Century as
Seasons of My Life (1989) and
Daughter of the Dales (1990)

This edition first published in 1991 by
Random Century Group Ltd, Random Century House,
20 Vauxhall Bridge Road, London SW1V 2SA

Random Century Australia (Pty) Ltd,
20 Alfred Street, Milsons Point,
Sydney 2061, Australia

Random Century New Zealand Ltd,
18 Poland Road, Glenfield,
Auckland 10, New Zealand

Random Century South Africa (Pty) Ltd,
PO Box 337, Bergvlei, 2012 South Africa

Reprinted 1991, 1992

A catalogue record for this book is
available from the British Library

ISBN 0 7126 5114 4

Design by Behram Kapadia

Typeset by Deltatype Ltd, Ellesmere Port

Printed and bound in Great Britain by
Butler & Tanner Ltd, Frome and London

Contents

Part One
Seasons of My Life

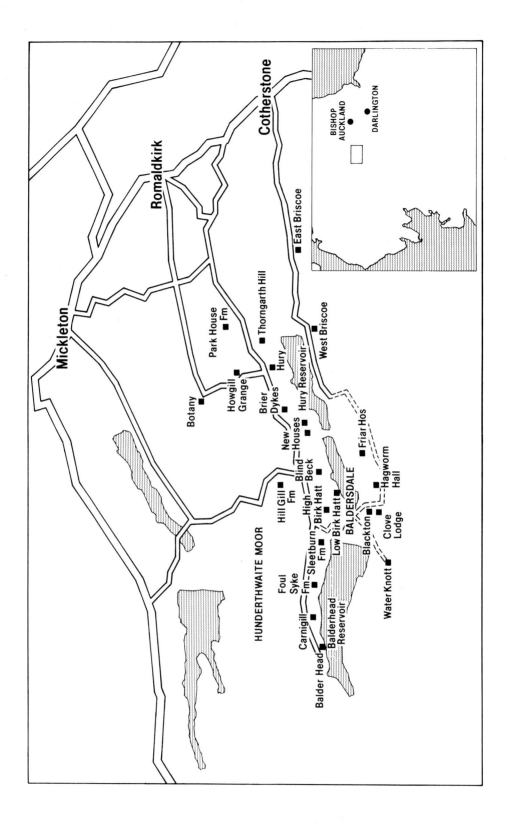

Preface

As she speaks, the cadences are clearly rooted in another time . . . a more mannered time. Late eighteenth or early nineteenth century perhaps. One thing is certain, however, when Hannah Hauxwell speaks, people listen. She possesses a quality which cannot properly be defined.

She talks guilelessly about her abiding love for her surroundings. Low Birk Hatt Farm lies in the desolate and partially abandoned sweep of Baldersdale, high in the Pennines. It is frequently uncomfortable in summer and a bleak prison sentence in winter. But to Hannah, whatever the physical discomforts, it is an enchanted land.

She puts her feelings into words, a strangely compelling, rhythmic web of sentences, and her listeners are obviously captivated. Hard-bitten and unsentimental they are, too, like all much travelled and overprivileged film crews. But their highly polished veneer of cynicism dissolves under the wash of a curious tide of articulate innocence.

It's my favourite place, here . . . down the new road through the iron gate. I stand here and watch the seasons come and go. At night the moonlight plays on Hunder Beck . . . and the waters sing a song to me . . .

I know this place will always be loyal to me. If I have nothing in my pocket I will always have this. They cannot take it away from me. It's mine, mine for the taking, and always will be . . . even when I'm no longer here.

A significant pause, and Hannah looks away over the glistening waters. When she turns back her eyes are flooding with tears. The film crew is stilled, like a freeze frame. Hannah recovers, smiles tremulously and concludes . . .

Hannah enjoys the view

LEFT: *Hury Reservoir, Baldersdale: a view from the road leading to Low Birk Hatt* (North Yorkshire County Library)

Of course, I suppose I shall have to leave here . . . sooner rather than later, I imagine. It will not be an easy thing to do.

But in years to come, if you see a ghost walking here you can be sure it will be me.

Hannah falls silent, and smiles again. Slowly, the film crew emerge from their trance. Those who know her never fail to wonder at the remarkable effect she has on people, however grand, whatever their background.

Of course, Hannah loves to talk because she rarely has the opportunity of conversation, of engaging an audience. She lives alone, a true castaway of life . . . trapped by circumstances in the sepia squalor of Low Birk Hatt.

She has the animals, her only constant companions. Her family she calls them . . . and they are outrageously indulged, from the indisciplined dog through to the irritable old cow. They all have names and she talks to them as though they are human. As conversations go they are a trifle one-sided, but nine days out of ten they are all she has. Low Birk Hatt must be the loneliest place in the Kingdom. They are so special to her, these dumb and clumsy beasts, that she can talk sorrowfully about some which departed for the glue factory decades ago.

Oh, and can she talk, this simple, ragged lady of the high Pennines. The words are soft and gentle but they can penetrate the soul. Which other ordinary, workaday person, someone who has achieved nothing in life by the standards laid down by society, has had two enormously successful, internationally networked film documentaries made about her, and is even now in the process of making a *third?*

She has left her isolation just twice in her sixty-two years – once to be a guest of honour at the 'Women of the Year' lunch at the Savoy Hotel (where she was besieged by Press and celebrities, including the wife of the then Prime Minister, plus minor royalty) and once to a Buckingham Palace garden party.

The third film may create the biggest impact of all. For this time she is going to leave Low Birk Hatt permanently . . . has to. If she stops the process she has so reluctantly started – the valuation of her land and cattle, the perusal of cottages for sale in the nearby villages – then the likely consequences do not bear contemplation . . . to be found dead, one killing winter, lying on the frozen stone slabs of her kitchen floor, partly eaten by rats.

Whatever happens, any television programme about Hannah will generate a great deal of emotion. She has countless devotees, who flood her farm with letters and presents and create serious space problems.

In the meantime, she talks . . . fascinatingly, poetically, about the seasons of her life. Her childhood . . . chapel . . . the horses that once worked the farm . . . the birds and wildlife . . . the changes wrought by the seasons . . . grandparents, uncles and aunts . . . the loneliness and hardships after all her relatives die . . . music and poetry appreciation as taught by her mother.

Here are all the reference points of life through the eyes and emotions of Hannah Bayles Tallentire Hauxwell . . . the lady with the inspirational quality which defies analysis.

Introduction

The message on my desk from a Yorkshire Television researcher was brief and very much to the point:

'Some friend of mine hiking the Pennine Way met a woman called Hannah Hauxwell living alone on an isolated farm in Baldersdale. No electricity, no water, good talker, could be worth a look!'

Alone, with neither water nor electricity? It was early summer in 1972 and I was putting together ideas for a series tentatively titled 'The Hard Life'. This lady's life sounded pretty hard.

Since the opening of Yorkshire Television in 1968 I had been working the Yorkshire Dales as often as possible. Urban life had no appeal for me so I began to make short films among the hill farmers and other Dales characters for inclusion in *Calendar*, the daily news and current affairs programme for the region we served. This thread developed into a regional series of twenty-to-thirty-minute programmes called *Country Calendar*, which had an immediate and very gratifying impact on the viewers. The local Press began to comment very favourably, and *Yorkshire Life* magazine even invited me to write about my films. Other independent television stations began to transmit them, so gradually they went network, coast to coast across the country.

Consequently, the head of the documentary department, John Fairley, and I sat down to try and analyse what it was about *Country Calendar* which had appealed to the public. What was the essence? John Fairley pinpointed it ... it appeared in his judgement that it was to do with hardship and loneliness. Sequences featuring shepherds spilling sweat on the fells, Dalesfolk suffering extremes of weather as a matter of course, small people in a huge, beautiful but often hazardous landscape had excited the interest of viewers and television journalists

14

alike. A phenomenally large postbag reinforced this view. So I was charged to seek out more Dalesfolk who lived a hard and lonely life. I briefed researchers in the department to let me know if they picked up any leads.

Thus, when I am asked (and it happens frequently) how I ever managed to find Hannah Hauxwell, a totally unknown figure at the top of an isolated and mainly abandoned Yorkshire dale, I can honestly say that I was, in a way, specifically looking for her, or people like her.

I very nearly didn't find her, as it turned out. That memo on my desk led me to the bottom of Baldersdale on one blustery July day. It looked a very empty place. Driving slowly along I came across a solitary figure examining the quality of his grass (it was nearly time to cut the hay) and solicited his aid.

'Hannah Hauxwell? Eh, lad! She lives at a place called Low Birk Hatt, but it's right near the top of the dale. Tha'll nivver find 'er!'

But I kept trying. I travelled some miles further along a road which wound sinuously along a truly attractive dale (and by then I was something of a connoisseur) augmented by the glistening waters of what I took to be a lake (it was actually Hury Reservoir, which wanders at length). Then I came across a sign which marked the Pennine Way, but it was pointing towards the high moors, where only Swaledale sheep can survive. Clearly that was the wrong way, so I began to follow the route in the opposite direction, abandoning the car when the unmown grass and rutted track began to scrape heavily against the exhaust system. By necessity, I had to climb over several dry stone walls which were crumbling from a generation's neglect, dislodging the occasional half hundredweight on to my shins, and came to a ridge. The prospect it revealed was distinctly unpromising. I could see two farmsteads in the distance, and both appeared to be abandoned. The sky had darkened ominously, and the kind of keen breeze which presages rain sprang up.

I considered the situation carefully, and came close to abandoning the project and seeking prospects other than this Hannah Hauxwell from a fairly long list. But I plunged over yet another trembling dry stone wall and chose, for no particular reason, to head for the farm on the left.

The nearer I approached, the less promising it became. There was no smoke issuing from the chimneys, the paths were overgrown, the slate roof of the barn was in a state of disrepair, and there was neither sight nor sound of life.

Quite suddenly a curious figure appeared from the rear of the farmhouse and began walking towards a pile of stone in the middle of the side pasture. A woman with hair as white as a pensioner's, wearing what appeared to be several layers of carefully laundered rags. It was a sight which stopped me short. I watched spellbound for a moment – she hadn't noticed me – then cleared my throat and said 'Er . . . Miss Hauxwell?'

She reacted like a roe deer on hearing an approaching predator, appearing to levitate about two feet in the air. I thought for an instant that she was going to flee across the fields, taking the boundary walls in her stride. I was not aware at this time that her life was so solitary that she could go two weeks without seeing a soul.

Hastily, I explained who I was, and the nature of my visit. She relaxed immediately and smiled in that seraphic way which would later transfer to celluloid and stir the emotions of a large section of the English-speaking world. The greeting she extended was delightfully antiquated, almost Victorian, in its mannerisms. She talked animatedly, clearly eager for conversation, and showed me around her house as she innocently described an extraordinary lifestyle, totally devoid of the comforts and standards everyone else takes for granted. The farmhouse was lit by oil lamps, the water was drawn from a stream running forty yards from her front door. Further upstream, a cow up to its hocks in the same water . . .

A couple of mesmeric hours later, I bade her farewell, and began the long trek back to Leeds and the Yorkshire Television studios. This time I knew I had a film from the Yorkshire Dales which would go straight on to the network.

But nobody at that stage, however fevered the imagination, could have forecast the impact Hannah Bayles Tallentire Hauxwell would have on the public.

16

Hannah in her carefully laundered rags

1

Baldersdale – A Classic Yorkshire Dale

Baldersdale, one of the tributary valleys of Teesdale, has been home to the various branches of the Hauxwell family for several (maybe countless) generations. It is a Yorkshire dale in a classic sense with sweeping contours and a fierce beauty on the grand scale, although in recent years it has been placed in County Durham (not that locals pay any attention to such cultural vandalism). But Baldersdale does have one extra visual blessing rarely seen in the Dales – water. Hury Reservoir was built a century or so ago and it stretches sinuously up a major portion of the valley. The eastern fells are reflected along its surface by day and the moon by night. The only other substantial piece of water in the western dales is Lake Semer Water, near Bainbridge, in Upper Wensleydale.

Baldersdale possesses another significant factor – it is a closed place. You can enter from the main road running along Teesdale but there is no way through at the top of the dale, unless you travel on horseback, or on foot, if you possess the stamina and know how to use a compass. No one just passes through Baldersdale, and this clearly played a major part in preserving its isolation in the days when it was a full and vibrant community, as, indeed, it certainly was. Today the place echoes with emptiness, its brown stone dwellings and farmhouses mainly abandoned, some neglected and crumbling, others no longer in existence. There are no children to educate so the schoolhouse is now a youth centre, the chapel no longer has its worshippers, the pub is now a farm.

But Hannah can vividly recall Baldersdale in its finest days, as a place where the full theatre of life was played out. She can even

Baldersdale (North Yorkshire County Library)

recall the minutiae which put flesh on the bones of memory – speech mannerisms, individual eccentricities and habits, clothing, names (even nicknames) hairstyles . . . everything. She builds up a full and fascinating portrait of a community with an acute sense of history which gives her descriptions a unique dimension.

As Hannah moves fluently along her journey into the past, what emerges most strongly to the listener is a sense of privilege – that here is a survivor of a lost way of life which was so innocent and simple, so materially deprived, yet spiritually rich, that it might have been part of another civilization altogether, surviving from an earlier century, perhaps. Such was their isolation that their way of life hardly reflected at all the kind to be found just a dozen miles away. Baldersdale was largely unaffected by contact with outside influences – to travel further than Barnard Castle, a prim and pretty little market town which could scarcely claim to be cosmopolitan, was virtually unheard of, and such visitors as there were never stayed long enough to impart revolutionary new ways and ideas. The horse and not the internal combustion engine provided the principal method of transport, and day-to-day living was based on unremitting toil and self-sacrifice. The land they tilled and the animals they raised absorbed most of their working hours. It was a constant battle, fuelled by the basic survival instinct which kept men moving ahead over thousands of years towards what we are pleased to call modern civilization today. In Baldersdale that process gathered no speed at all and indeed, never even crossed the finishing line.

The entire community was also welded together by two other elements. The knowledge that the only help you could expect in times of trouble or need would have to be sought from a near neighbour; and, even more fundamental, the bond of blood. Dalesfolk around the first half of the century tended to marry within their close community, so nearly everyone was related to nearly everyone else. Hannah's parents were half cousins and there were many convoluted relationships. For instance, in Chapter Five of this book Hannah records that her piano teacher's father and her, that is Hannah's, grandmother were cousins! How on earth that evolved is probably a relativity equation comparable with Einstein's.

A century ago, Baldersdale had a population numbering several hundred and supported a blacksmith, two pubs and even a small flour mill. It had declined substantially by the late thirties but was still a thriving place compared with the Baldersdale of today.

Oh yes, Baldersdale was a busy place in my childhood, full of people. There was always someone in the next field to say 'Hello' to, and the school, which had two teachers, usually had more than thirty children in attendance. There must have been more than twenty farms, plus the school, the chapel and the Strathmore Arms. They used to hold Hury Show in a field alongside the pub, and there was a wooden hut called the Show Room to be used on the big day, where dances were also held on a regular basis.

Low Birk Hatt Farm has always been home for my family. No one else has ever lived here. Although I was born at Sleetburn further up the dale, I came here when I was three years old, so I do not recall any other place as home. We used to rent it from the Kipling family before Daddy bought it, but even my great-grandfather William Bayles farmed at Low Birk Hatt.* It was a mixed farm, with cattle, sheep and geese. I remember my uncle Tommy Hauxwell, who came to live with us to manage the farm after Father died, telling me about the time Great-Grandad bought a big flock of geese over in Stainmore, which is more than six miles away over the moors. And he drove them home all the way, presumably with the help of his dogs. Uncle said he will never forget as a little boy the sight of all these geese coming over the hill beyond our top pasture.

He must have been quite an enterprising businessman, my great-grandad, because he ran the butter cart in Baldersdale. It was red in colour and had much bigger wheels than the ordinary farm cart. A mare called Smiler used to pull it, and he would collect all the butter and eggs in the dale to take to

---

* The Kiplings probably built and certainly owned Low Birk Hatt, but never lived there, according to Hannah.

Hury Show, Baldersdale (Beamish, North of England Open Air Museum)

Buttermaking at Cotherstone (Beamish)

Barnard Castle. He would call on some farms and others would bring what they had to sell down to Low Birk Hatt. I've heard that this farm was a very busy place on Tuesday nights and Wednesday mornings and the kitchen would be piled high with eggs and butter. Then Great-Grandad would drive the lot down to Barnard Castle to get the best price he could in the market place.

People would turn up again in large numbers on Wednesday nights to be paid for their produce. Naturally Great-Grandad would take a share, a sort of commission for his trouble, if you like. And he would bring back goods from the market, such as meal, and sell or exchange that for what the Dalesfolk had brought. The old system of barter I suppose.

Great-Grandfather was running a farm at the same time, so he must have been a very busy man. And life was quite a struggle for everyone, it seems. I'm going back now to before

24

the First World War, sometime in the early years of this century. But I do know that when times were bad, the people in the dale had to use the wool off the backs of the sheep themselves instead of sending it away to the wool merchants of Bradford after shearing. They would make more money that way.

We had a spinning wheel at Low Birk Hatt – it may be still around the place somewhere – and the whole family would spin the raw wool and then knit it into stockings, gloves, jumpers and skirts. I do believe that in years gone by they paid the annual rent for Low Birk Hatt by spinning and knitting.

Eventually the Kiplings put Low Birk Hatt up for sale and there is a sad and curious story associated with this. It concerns my great-aunt Jane Bayles, who was my father's mother's sister and lived at Hury at the bottom of the dale. She was both a clever woman and a fool at one and the same time. Her sister, my great-aunt Margaret Bayles, married a Dales-man called George Brown, and lived at Blackton Farm. They hired a man with red hair called John Bell to catch the moles which were plaguing their land. From what I can gather he was as mad as a hatter, and really no good at all. He was what we called 'a hook', which means a slippery fish.

Anyway, Great-Aunt Jane shared everyone's low opinion of John Bell for a time, even going as far as to declare that he wasn't right in his head. And then, would you believe it, she went and married him. I gather from the little bits of information which came my way that the match was a disaster. I do know that he outlived Great-Aunt Jane and he made a lot of trouble by claiming items of property to which he had no right. He brought nothing at all into the marriage, and the family wanted nothing to do with him. I heard that Uncle Tommy was in Barnard Castle one day when someone asked him, 'Are ye owt 'a kin to yon John Bell?' Uncle denied it and when challenged said, 'Aye, he might have wed my aunt but that doesn't mek 'm owt 'a kin to me.' He was a real pest, and thank goodness he and Great-Aunt Jane had no children.

But Great-Aunt Jane did a very strange thing. My father and mother were living at Sleetburn, where I was born, with my

Great-Aunt Jane Bayles and Great-Uncle William Bayles in Birk Hatt

grandparents and a great-uncle, when Low Birk Hatt came up for auction. Daddy wanted that farm very badly but they didn't have much money between them, so he had to go to the bank and ask for a loan. And then – what a lunatic thing to do – Great-Aunt Jane began to bid against my father at the auction for Low Birk Hatt. Uncle Tommy always said that there was insanity in the family, so that incident proves it, if nothing else.

Goodness only knows why she did it, but it put the price up, of course. It was knocked down to Father for £1,600, which in those days – it was the 1920s – was a very high price. I do know that he became very depressed when the times were bad and he had the mortgage payments to meet. It was a great struggle for him and we all suffered because of it.

Oddly enough my father allowed Great-Aunt Jane and John Bell to live at Low Birk Hatt after he had bought it. I cannot imagine why. But I do know *that* great-aunt was not exactly popular after the incident of the farm sale, and eventually John Bell left her so her brother, Great-Uncle William, came to work the farm.

It was always considered necessary for a man to shoulder the main burden of work at a farm the size of ours, and I suppose the main reason why the place is a bit run down these days is because there was no man left to take over when Uncle died. I had to do it all by myself.

2

Portrait of an Enclosed Community

As these family dramas were played out around Low Birk Hatt Farm and the Hauxwell family battled against the twin effects of an overpriced, heavily mortgaged farm, and an agricultural depression which presaged the deep national depression of the thirties, the other people in Baldersdale coped with their lives. Hannah recalls the people, the personalities and the events in fine detail.

Balder Head was the highest farm in the dale, as the name suggests, and a family called Green lived there. Husband and wife and three boys, and later on they had a little girl. It was a small farm and I think Mr Green had to work away from home sometimes to bring a bit more money in. I do believe it was forestry work that he did.

The boys were younger than me but I remember them coming to school – and what a job that was for them. They had to walk, and a real hike it was – getting on for three miles I think. Eventually their father came to some arrangement with the Education Authority and he was able to afford a small car to drive them to school.

I only went once to visit the Greens and then I was collecting money for the Missionary Fund to which most people contributed a copper or two, with young Mrs Thwaites from the neighbouring farm to us, High Birk Hatt. Balder Head farmhouse was so close to the reservoir that the water lapped up to the garden wall. The place is no longer there now, but it wasn't one of the several that fell down after being abandoned. It was taken away stone by stone and rebuilt in part at

The Addisons of Carnigill

the Beamish Museum in the Newcastle area, which specializes in preserving country ways. So Balder Head must have had some architectural significance or other, although I doubt if anyone in the dale realized it.

The next farm down was West Carnigill where Mr and Mrs Addison, Jack and Madge, lived. Mrs Addison was a bonny woman with a mass of dark hair which she wore in a coil. Sadly she wasn't blessed with good health – in fact, neither was Mr Addison – and they had no children. But they stayed the longest in Baldersdale, apart from me of course, and eventually retired down to Hunderthwaite, down near the main road.

Near to them was East Carnigill and the Bellerbys. They had three children, Doris who was a bit older than me, Jim a bit younger, and a little chap called Ernest. Doris and Jim went to school at the same time as me.

Then there was Foul Syke, where a man called Lance Sowerby lived. I have a feeling that he had been married but I do not know what happened. I used to see him at Chapel Anniversary, and my uncle would say that he was a romancer, meaning that in the nicer way. He could spin a yarn, and you had to take what he said with a pinch of salt.

After that came Sleetburn, where I was born on 1 August 1926, which was owned by a William Hutchinson when we lived there. We were followed by Mr and Mrs Atkinson, their son Douglas, and Mrs Atkinson's two sisters, the Misses Elizabeth and Annabella Hind. Now this was a family I was very close to eventually when they became quite near neighbours in later years by moving to Clove Lodge, just up the pasture from Low Birk Hatt. I used to go and stay there at Christmastime, after Father died, and there was always a nice present on the juniper tree for me and lots of good things to eat. We had stopped celebrating Christmas in the proper manner after Father died. I suppose we really couldn't afford to.

They had been followed to Sleetburn by the Wilkinson family, who had moved from West Thorngarth Hill down the dale at Hury because they needed a bigger farm, I seem to remember. They had a son and a daughter, Sidney and Agnes.

Well now we come to West Birk Hatt and the Fawcett family, and really wonderful people they were. Such a lot of them too, with eight children, as well as a resident relative. Let me see, there would be Mary and Ellen, two older daughters who were soon to move away, and then Neddy, Sidney, George, Dick, Sepp, and eventually Geoffrey. Sepp was really Septimus, the seventh, and I called one of my calves the same name.

Mr Sam Fawcett was a truly remarkable man, and if he were alive today would be a television and radio personality, I am

Sam Fawcett

certain. Indeed he did broadcast on the BBC before the war with a man called Harry Hopeful who ran a very popular show, rather on the same lines as Wilfrid Pickles and his *Have a Go* programme. Sam could sing and play the concertina and violin, and he must have been good for the BBC to come all the way to Baldersdale to find him. I wonder how that happened.

I know he would regularly come down to Low Birk Hatt – and, indeed, Sleetburn when we were there – with his violin, and Mother used to accompany him on our organ. They spent hours together, particularly when one or the other had acquired a new piece of music. I recall one man in the dale saying that he passed Sleetburn going up the fell to shepherd at 10 a.m. one day and heard Sam and Mother playing. He came back at 3 p.m. and they were still going.

Wherever the Fawcetts were you would hear music. It was lovely on the hot summer nights listening to the sound of the various instruments being played at West Birk Hatt, drifting half a mile across the valley. Sam had a bachelor brother called Tom, known as Tuck, who had silver hair and beard. He was a very good sheep man and had been known to tap dance, but only on very rare and special occasions.

Sam was also a keen and talented naturalist. What he didn't know about birds, foxes, moles and all the other creatures of the fields wasn't worth knowing. Of course, he had been brought up to it because his father, Edmund Fawcett, was a gamekeeper. That was before my time, of course, but he obviously passed on some of his skills because during, or just after, very wet weather, Sam would go off somewhere and catch lovely brown trout, which he often gave to people who were ill; and sometimes when he had a sheep to kill, he would send down the head which would make a really tasty and nourishing broth. His garden was a credit to him, too, and he grew flowers and potatoes. He would also give those away, and I remember when my poor father died he brought down one, if not two, lovely lilies which Mother put in a slender silver vase. He was such a loyal, staunch and tender-hearted friend of my family, and such an outgoing man. He laughed a lot and his laugh would boom down the dale. He used to come over to us a lot at weekends, along with another character called Bob Brown, who lived at Blackton and who was a bachelor brother of my great-aunt's husband. He was a very decent man but had not been blessed with all the faculties one would normally expect.

Anyway they would land down at our place most weekends, because we used to take the *Darlington and Stockton Times*, and they would all be smoking their pipes and talking, asking, 'What hast thou fresh, now' and catching up on the comings and goings of Baldersdale. They were grand folk, and it's because of them that I am not one of the antismoking lobby (although I have never associated personally with nicotine). It's just that I have such happy pictures in my mind of those times that pipes will always have nice associations for me.

Another thing we had which would attract the locals to call was a weather glass – a barometer most people would call it, I suppose, and I still have it on my wall. They would visit to see what it was doing at particular times, like haymaking.

Mrs Fawcett, Sam's wife, was another grand person. She and Mother were the best of friends, and she knew that I was daft over dollies and wanted one so badly. Anyhow, she set to and found the time to make one for me, even though she had such a large family to care for. The body was made from the strong cotton bags that the flour came in, she worked some black fur for its hair, and stuffed it with straw or some old hay. Then with her needle she worked eyebrows, eyes and mouth, and made a dress out of an old dress that belonged to one of her girls. I can picture it now, a fine velvet cord and such bonny colours. Septimus brought it down for me one Christmastime when I was just a girl – before the last war anyhow. Septimus was younger than me and not very big and he could scarcely carry this big lovely dolly. I cherished that dolly, kept on altering the face with new stitching from time to time and I still have it in a drawer somewhere.

I really do not know where Mrs Fawcett found the energy to do what she did. I seem to recall that she baked a stone of flour a week making bread and teacakes to keep all those mouths fed. I heard that she lost one baby as well, and I do know that she suffered badly with her legs, varicose veins, I believe. Sad thing was she had been a noted dancer in her day. It was quite usual to see her standing there baking, one knee on a cushion placed on a stool, to ease the pain.

I have very affectionate memories of Sidney, one of the elder Fawcett boys. Uncle got a white dog from him once, a very unusual colour for a farm dog. It was exchanged later for a black Old English sheepdog owned by some relatives of ours at Piercebridge. Sidney pretended to be upset about this – at least I think he was pretending –because he said to Uncle, 'A 's not friends wi' thee now – thee's parted wi' my white dog'.

Sidney was a tall young man like his brother George. When war came in 1939, Sidney went into the Coldstream Guards and George into the Grenadier Guards. They would come

Sidney Fawcett

back on leave and wear their scarlet tunics in the dale. I can see them in my mind's eye even now. They were grand boys and so courageous . . . maybe too much so as it turned out.

You see, I'm sad to say that Sidney never came back. He was taken prisoner in Italy and tried to escape, I understand. The Fawcett family were very brave about it when the telegram came from the War Office. Oh dear, that was a black day in Baldersdale. Believe me, we all had a warm place in our hearts for Sidney.

George was taken prisoner, too, when he was fighting in France, and I remember reading in a newspaper how he had escaped as well. He had been at large in occupied France and had quite a tough time of it, but at least he survived and came back to Baldersdale.

Mind, the Fawcett family's association with the dale had a sad ending, because Mr Fawcett died, and then their farm, West Birk Hatt, disappeared when they built the extension to the reservoir at Balder Head. What's left of it is many yards under water now.

The closest people to us in terms of distance were the Thwaites, just at the top of our main pasture, in High Birk Hatt. Here again the lady of the house was so kind and resourceful. The husband was called Jack, and everyone called him by his first name, but for some reason one always called his wife Mrs Thwaites, although we all knew her Christian name was Margaret. It was just one of those things that you cannot explain.

They had two daughters, Violet and Madge, and two sons, Luther and John. Both girls were keen cyclists and since they lived near the road they could get out and about. They both married, with Madge going to live in Cotherstone, just about the nearest village to us, and Violet staying near the bottom of the dale. Luther did leave the community for good, going off to work in Darlington, where he married and settled down.

When the elders at our place began to fall ill, Mrs Thwaites was the best neighbour we could have. She was such a hard worker and a wonderful cook. She would send over beef tea and other delicacies to try and cheer them up. They were good

Margaret Thwaites

to me, too, and I recall young John Thwaites being sent down to our farm one Christmas with such a big rosy red apple that I can close my eyes and still see it now. And when I went to play occasionally near to their house, Mrs Thwaites would bring out large sweet biscuits for me. She was really good at baking.

We had four elderly people to look after at Low Birk Hatt, my father's parents and two uncles. That meant that there were seven mouths to feed, and then Daddy began to ail.

When the elder members of the family began to die, Mrs Thwaites did most, if not all of the baking and catering for the funerals. The undertaker was Mr Alan Anderson from the firm of Raines, joiners of Mickleton, who would carry out his duties with great delicacy, sympathy and understanding.

The Thwaites of High Birk Hatt

We used to get our hay rakes from the same firm, and they were so beautifully made – light and easy to work with. I still have one or two but they are near the end of their useful life.

There was another family in the dale which, like us, lost their father and mainstay at an early age. They were the Sayers over at West New Houses, a big place with a sheep moor which belonged to the Strathmores, the Queen Mother's family.

It was a big undertaking, this farm, with hired hands on a permanent basis, so they were pretty well off by the standards of Baldersdale. Mr and Mrs Sayers had five children, but only one son, John. Then Mr Sayers died prematurely when John was only about fifteen, so he was still just a boy when he had to become a man overnight, so to speak, and try and take on the running of this large and rather complicated farm. The entire future of the family and the farm fell on his shoulders, and what a wonderful job he made of it. He was always so quick witted and courageous was John that I always thought he would have made a good secret agent – a James Bond kind of figure. He had such energy and drive, and liked to play hard as well as work hard, and had a few scrapes with his motorbike. The girls were called Lizzie, Winnie, Ada and Edith, and I think all of them got married. John married later on, too.

Over at Hill Gill Farm there was another lady who had musical talent – Mrs Annie Bainbridge. This was a rather isolated place, tucked behind a hill and she used to run a little shop, probably for the company as much as anything. I know she became somewhat lonely because her husband, although he was a very hard worker, would go off on a spree for some days at a time. They weren't badly off because I do believe they ran a car and she would wear a lovely fox fur when she was out and about in the dale. She would wear it for Chapel Anniversary, I would think, because that was a very special occasion in Baldersdale. I can still bring it to mind, with lines of people coming off the hillsides and on to the road. They would bring their relations, too, and there would always be visiting preachers and singers who used to stay in the dale – we would always find room for our special visitors.

The chapel was only a single-storey affair and for anniversaries and other big events they used to make extra seats by placing bars of wood between one seat and the next. I used to enjoy the singing a lot but sometimes the preachers used to go on quite a bit. Just when you thought they were about to finish they would burst off again. It was too much for a little girl and I think it rather put me off chapel. And then we would get the evangelists staying for a fortnight at a time, holding services every night asking people to come forward and rededicate themselves. I have to say I didn't really care much for that kind of approach.

ABOVE: *Baldersdale Methodist chapel* (Northern Echo)
BELOW: *The plaque above the doorway of Baldersdale Methodist chapel*
(Northern Echo)

Then in wintertime we had a Guild meeting every Tuesday night with various people taking turns to organize it. I would recite some of the lines Grandad had taught me and sometimes sing songs like 'Who Will Buy My Pretty Flowers'. Once after I had recited at the Guild I was given a pair of woollen gloves, speckled coloured, and with cuffs, which was quite an unexpected treat.

The chapel is closed nowadays, and the school is a youth

Baldersdale school with Mrs Archer

centre. At one time there would be more than thirty children
and two teachers. The senior was Mrs Archer who lived in the
schoolhouse with her husband and daughter, Bessie, who
joined the ATS in the war. She was assisted by Miss Walker,
whom I liked very much, and I was so sad when she left to get
married.

Hannah's class. Hannah is second from left, middle row

Now Mrs Archer was a very good woman in her way but I'm afraid that I was never one of her favourites because I was so slow to catch on, particularly in mathematics. I cannot say that my school days were particularly happy ones and I was not

sorry to leave when I got to the official leaving age, which was fourteen in those days.

That was not long after the Second World War broke out. But I was still at school when the evacuees arrived mostly from Newcastle and Sunderland, so they would be safe from German air raids. They brought one or two of their own teachers with them, and farms which had the room to spare took them in as boarders.

The schoolchildren were split into seven standards or classes but we only had one room and one blackboard. It must have been difficult for the teachers to organize things even before the arrival of the evacuees, who had problems of their own, of course, adjusting to a major change in lifestyle. We would be split into different groups, with perhaps ten sitting round the blackboard for one lesson and the others in another part of the room working at something else. There were two fireplaces, one at each end of the classroom, two large cupboards and the teacher's desk was on the north wall.

The school day always began with prayers at nine o'clock, followed by a scripture lesson, and there was invariably arithmetic in some form or another until dinnertime. The rest of the time was devoted to history or geography, but always there would be two afternoons given over to handicrafts, particularly knitting and sewing. Even the boys had to knit. We also had looms and were taught weaving, basketwork and raffia. The day finished at 3.30 p.m.

We took our own sandwiches for lunch and a teacher would boil a kettle so we could make tea or cocoa for ourselves. There was no need for free milk like other school children received, because most of us came from farms with cows, so we brought our own.

There weren't many facilities for games, but the boys used to kick a football about the yard, and the girls played rounders. In later years some swings were put up for the school, but that was after my time.

Of course I enjoyed the company at school because my childhood was a bit lonely. There were no brothers and sisters for me to play with, and the only one I could really call a playmate was Derek Brown who lived just ten minutes away from Low Birk Hatt at Blackton Farm. Derek's mother was my great-aunt's daughter which I think made him a half cousin to me. He used to call for me to go to school, and that could be an eventful journey because the way led through the Sayers' farm at West New Houses, and they kept a flock of geese and a bull.

They were careful to keep the bull in the same field much of the time but sometimes they would have to move him and occasionally he would get out, so one always had to be wary. But I was also terrified of the geese because of a childhood experience – I was chased by a flock and the memory always stayed with me. They can really hurt you, particularly the ganders because they have such strong wings. So it was rather a question of running the gauntlet when passing over the Sayers' land. Trouble was I could never run very quickly, and I cannot imagine what I would have done if I had been chased by the bull. Now they are really dangerous and I understand that even today they are responsible for a number of deaths and serious accidents each year among farm workers. As far as I can recall there were no unfortunate incidents involving animals in Baldersdale. Bad weather took more of a toll in our community and Derek Brown's family suffered a tragedy during one bad winter. Their only son at the time, a cousin of my father's called William Bayles Brown, went out on Cotherstone Moor in a snow storm to gather up some sheep, and never came back. A search party found him the next day, dead from exposure. They could tell from his footprints in the snow that he had been trying to find a fold, which is what we call a stone shelter built for gathering sheep. His body was found very close to it, but he had obviously been blinded by the blizzard. He may have survived if only he could have found it. The poor man left a widow and a young daughter.

A newspaper account of this incident makes fascinating reading, written as it is in the florid, expansive style of the day to extract every ounce of drama. It was a triple headline: 'Tragic Death on a Teesdale Moor' . . . 'Shepherd Vanquished in a Raging Storm' . . . 'Fateful Vigil of a Sheepdog'. It goes on:

'The story of the death of William Bayles Brown, only son of George and Margaret Brown of Blackton, Baldersdale, is a weird narrative of the melancholy end of a courageous shepherd on a high moor in Teesdale . . . at eleven o'clock last Thursday morning the deceased left home in an endeavour to bring the high moor sheep to shelter . . . went off, whistling aloud, in the direction of the ill-fated higher common. He was soon fully a mile on the moor, a terrible doom, forsooth, awaiting him. There had been a phenomenally heavy snowstorm in Baldersdale, and especially on the loftier peaks. There were found footprint evidences that young Brown had crossed and recrossed Hunder Beck, that he had been at the top of the high moor, and he was traced half way back, with probably thirty-six sheep which were recovered on Sunday. It was in the gloaming on Thursday that the brave young fellow's father became alarmed by reason of his son not returning, and the distressed parent went to see a neighbour. As a matter of fact, he called upon Mr Fawcett and unburthened [sic] his apprehensions . . . Deceased's father, with Thomas Hawkswell [sic] set out as a search party, and eventually traced the "footings" of the missing man . . . to the old Groove house, and found the lifeless body of young Brown lying just outside the dilapidated building, with his faithful dog watching over the remains of its departed master . . . the deceased had been married about nine months but he, however, resided with his father at Blackton, while his wife lived with her mother at Bowes, pending their securing a farm and home to themselves, a consummation well within sight at the time of this untoward happening –this mysterious interposition, which surely intimates eternity to man . . .'

The Bayles were quite plentiful in the dale for many years – my great-great-grandfather was a John Bayles – but they have all gone now, except me. I am the only one left in Baldersdale with Bayles blood in my veins.

The main branch of the Bayles family farmed at New Houses. The head of the family when I first remember them was William Henry Bayles who was Grandmother's cousin and the father of a lady who taught me a little bit of music. She was their only daughter. Then there was William Henry's wife Mary, and his niece, Mary Hannah, who unfortunately lost both parents when she was young and came to make her home with them. The farm had originally been two or three houses and there was a little cottage at the back where a lady we used to call Aunt Polly lived. She was William Henry's sister, and it was such a nice place. We would visit her on occasions and I remember she had a rather splendid grand-father clock. The Bayles and the Tallentires were related by marriage. Great-Great-Grandfather Tallentire had a daughter called Hannah who became a Bayles when she married and who was my father's grandmother. Her brother was William Tallentire and he became my mother's grandfather, which meant that my mother and father were akin. It probably made them half cousins. Then there was a great-great-grandmother Elizabeth Tallentire, who was Grandmother Bayles's mother, who lived with her husband at a farm over at Holwick, which is a little way out of Baldersdale, on the way to Middleton in Teesdale. Now Great-Great-Grandmother Elizabeth must have been a very capable woman because circumstances demanded that her husband went out to work as a miner, so she was left to manage the farm. And she had six children, three of each, yet still found time to appreciate music, a very strong trait of the Tallentires.

Sad to say that there was a disaster in her family too, which was once again caused by the weather. A group of people had just finished haytiming at a farm called Pikestone, in Holwick, and began to cross the swing bridge across the Tees. Apparently there must have been very heavy rain higher up the dale because there had been some flooding and the river was running very fast. The story goes that it was a very merry party – maybe they were celebrating being able to get in the hay after a bad spell – and they stepped on the bridge to enjoy some music, a very Tallentire thing to do. Anyhow the bridge collapsed and a number were drowned, including I believe, one of Great-Grandmother's sons, Thomas Tallentire.

Haymaking, now that was an important event in the life of the dale – still is for me – because that's when you harvest the fodder for the animals when winter comes and there is no grazing to be had. Lambing time is even more important because lambs are a cash crop and nobody ever had an abundance of that.

I can still hear in my imagination the sounds of lambing in springtime, particularly from Blind Beck, just over to the north-east from us where the Lowsons farmed. John and Elsie they were called, and they had two sons, Stanley and Gilbert. Grandfather Lowson lived with them – he was called Matthew, nicknamed Mather – and he was a character who could tell a good story.

The Lowsons were reckoned to be very good farmers and they were very up to date. There was such a racket from their

Haytime at West Park, Cotherstone (Beamish)

place at night during lambing time – and that's a twenty-four-hour job with no time to sleep. They had the modern aluminium racks on wheels for foddering the sheep instead of the traditional, very much more silent version made from wood. Well, the lids of these racks rattled like mad as they put the hay in to feed the sheep after they had given birth. So with that and all the shouting at each other and the dogs, lambing time was extremely noisy.

Mind the Lowsons stuck to the old ways in other respects. During wintertime John Lowson was rarely seen without his hessian sacks. Now the old-fashioned, strong hessian is wonderful for keeping you warm and dry and John always sported three sacks – one round his waist, another over his shoulders, and the third with the corner pushed in for a hood over his head.

The Lowsons farmed Blind Beck for a number of generations. John's grandmother, Betty Hind, lived there and she was quite famous in the dale as someone you did not trifle with. Not a battleaxe exactly but I hear she used to stomp around the place in clogs and speak her mind without fear or hesitation.

At the end of the reservoir dam there used to be a place called Blackton House which was rather crowded. It was where Fred Sowerby and his wife lived, and they had seven children, Teresa, Eric, Ruth, Gertie, Norman, Mabel and Pat. Mr Sowerby worked for the Water Board and unfortunately was permanently affected by an injury sustained in the First World War. There was some shrapnel in one of his legs which they had never been able to get out. Poor man, he dropped down dead just at the beginning of the terrible winter of 1947.

Sadly their house doesn't exist any more. It was just left abandoned like so many of the others and fell into a state of disrepair. The authorities decided it was dangerous so it had to be knocked down.

Another place across the dale from us was East New Houses, where a maiden lady lived when I was a child. She was Miss Sarah Anne Walker, an only child left to cope on her own when both her mother and father died. But the family had been comfortably off, and she was able to hire hands to run the farm. Anyhow, a man called Jack Foster, who came from round Middleton way, was employed as her farm manager, and ended up marrying Miss Walker. I remember the wedding and I do believe that Mr Foster was a bit younger than she, but he was a very sincere and deeply caring person. I do know that they were both very kind to their hired help and treated one or two more like sons than employees. They

The Walkers of Briar Dyke

would let them stay on until they married and got farms of their own, because, perhaps, their own home circumstances would not be very good. Miss Walker was a mature lady when she married, if my memory serves me correctly, and they never had children of their own.

There were some other Walkers at Brier Dykes who were related to Miss Sarah Anne. Thomas and Agnes Walker, they were called, and they had a son called Tommy, who was a good deal older than me, and two daughters who had married and left the dale before my memory of Baldersdale begins. They were God-fearing folk and attended Sunday services regularly, he a very quiet man, and she a rather stout and well-built lady. Tommy was married before the war and raised a family.

The Walkers of Briar Dyke

Over at the west end of Hury there was a house which had been a pub called the Hare and Hounds, occupied by a family who were rather special to me. There was a widow-lady called Mrs Raw and her son Bernard, who shared their home with an elderly gentleman, Mr William Wilkins. We used to call him Daddy Wilkins because he was the father of a large family, but they had all grown up, got married and spread about, so he was left on his own – probably not able to cook for himself which is why he went to live at Mrs Raw's place. She was such a nice, kind lady and I recall her taking care of me on one of the Sunday School trips when Mother was unable to go. And I had an affection for Bernard who went to school with me. Although he was three or four years older, he was always thoughtful and friendly towards me, never unkind, when, perhaps, some of the other pupils were not as pleasant. You see, I would be teased a lot at school because I may not have been as quick as the others, but Bernard never joined in. He had a favourite song he used to sing in the old days – 'It's a Sin to Tell a Lie' – and I shall always associate it with him.

Close to the Raws' was another house called Dovers where an elderly couple called Bell lived, and just over the wall from there was Nelson House where Grandfather and Grandmother Hauxwell lived before they moved to Sleetburn. The next family to occupy Nelson House was the Linds, who were friends of my family. They had a son William, and a daughter Margaret, and a niece of Mrs Lind called Marjorie also lived with them. The father, David, had two nice Dales horses called Bonnie and Bess, both good, thick-set animals. Mr Lind used to ride Bess and, on occasion, would lend us Bonnie. The Linds are resident at Nelson House even to this day. I'm afraid that William died, but his wife and son Keith are still there with Keith's wife, Maureen, and their daughter, Catherine.

Further along the north side of Baldersdale there's Thorn-garth Hill where the Wilkinsons lived before they moved to Sleetburn. They were followed by the Kiplings when they retired from Clove Lodge, which had been in the family for generations. The Kiplings owned both places – and Low Birk Hatt in the early days of course – so they were well off by local standards. Over the back was Howgill Grange, inhabited by another branch of the same Walker family mentioned previously. The father was John Henry Walker and there were two daughters, Ada and Florence. Ada was a particularly striking young lady, with a pale complexion contrasted by very dark hair.

Further up the same road there were even more Walkers, all related, living at Botany Farm – William and Annie with one daughter, Marjorie, who was a little bit older than me. We went to school together, went to the same dances and then she married a soldier during the war. He came from Cambridge, and I haven't heard of her for a number of years.

Then there was East Thorngarth Hill, and the Simpsons. They had just the one son, Cecil, but four daughters, Ella, Connie, Rance and Muriel. They were keen Chapel folk and used to bring masses of flowers to Sunday School Anniversary. I am sorry to say that some of them are dead now, and others have left the dale to live in Barnard Castle with their own families.

Of course, most people have left now – either died or moved away.

I'm afraid that's the story of Baldersdale today . . . the place they abandoned . . . the dale they left to die. No chapel, no school, no recreation room, no pub, no social life of any kind really. The place was so full once, alive with activity and children. Baldersdale is an empty place now and all that remains for me are memories, sweet memories.

3

'Too Long a Winter'

They called the film they made about me *Too Long a Winter*, and I have to declare immediately that I do not care for winter at all, for neither mind nor body agrees with it. You could say that most winters in Baldersdale are too long, and every time we have a really bad one it takes something away from me in a physical sense. Saps one's strength you could say. But if you are a farmer like me you cannot avoid winter, whatever your age or physical condition. The animals need foddering, so out you have to go, whether or not there's a storm brewing.

Of course, when one was a child many years ago winter could be an advantage, and if the storm was bad enough they had to close the school, which was wonderful. And I recall when I was much younger when women didn't wear trousers at all, the novelty of putting on Uncle's knee breeches, jacket and coat, to go out to the fields.

Nowadays I consider that winter comes too early in Baldersdale and stays too long. The last really bad one was in 1978 when the electricity was off for four days. I had not had the benefit of that lovely electricity for long, but how I did miss it when it absented itself. Everything in the house froze solid –the water in the kettle, even my false teeth in a cup beside my bed. And my coat, my big army coat, which is forty years old now but still a good friend, and as strong as ever, became a remarkable sight. It became very wet as I carried water to the beasts because there were some very rough days and then it flared out and froze. I looked just like a crinoline lady.

Having no power was the greatest problem. The chimney is blocked so I couldn't light a fire to heat anything up and I went without a hot drink for those four days. I did get a little warm milk from Rosa (but I am not at all keen on milk) and the warmest place at Low Birk Hatt, in fact, was the cow byre. I think it will be the hay that increases the temperature.

I would go straight to bed after finishing my work with all my clothes on, including Uncle's old tweed coat and socks. It was not an experience I would wish to endure very often.

I remember well the moment when the electricity came back on. At the time I was mucking out the byre stalls, and piling the manure on top of my big heap when I saw the lights go on in the house. I have had the pleasure of seeing some welcome sights in my time, but that comes very near the top of the list.

Mind, the worst winter of all was 1947. It never seemed to end. And the entire thing was preceded by a death at one of the near farms, just before the first of the storms came.

The frost was so hard that everything went steel grey – the ground, the water and the sky. The blizzards just went on and on, day after day, blowing the snow about. We had to dig out every day, and if you didn't hurry getting water and bringing the cattle out to drink, the path you had just made would be filled in again. Eventually the snow was so deep that it filled in all the fields with only the top few inches of the wall sticking out. Some of those walls were six feet in height. And the snow was so hard with the frost that you could walk over it with safety. That was just about the only redeeming feature of that winter because it formed a kind of bridge which made walking up to the road a lot easier. We had coal to carry from the top pasture by the road where the coalman used to leave it, and I don't think it would have been possible but for that snow bridge.

Of course, I was a lot younger and more able to cope in 1947, and I wasn't alone – Father had died by then but there was Mother and Uncle. I had to help Uncle fetch the coal for us and some corn oats for Prince the colt, and a mare which was in foal. We used a sledge with Prince pulling it along. And it was going downhill over the hard packed snow which was the worst bit, with me acting as a brake, hauling on a rope to keep the sledge from running forward into the horse's heels. The sheep had the worst time, and not many survived 1947, although provisions for people and animals alike were dropped in by helicopter, and the Army forced a way through on the south side of the dale.

The hardships produced a wonderful spirit in the community. Everybody would help everybody else. It became known that we were perilously short of hay because the haytiming on our pastures had been very poor that summer and it was impossible to bring enough in on the horse-drawn sledge on the few occasions we were able to get out. But neighbours sent down what they had to spare. And the people who were farming Blind Beck at the time killed a pig and sent down a lovely pork pie to us. There were several similar examples of true neighbourliness.

Then I was able to help when young Mrs Thwaites at High Birk Hatt, our nearest neighbours, suffered terribly from toothache and needed to go to the nearest dentist, who was in Barnard Castle. I offered to go with her for company and safety really, since it was dangerous to go out alone in conditions like that. Anyway, I knew what she was going through since I had been obliged to have all my top teeth out just before the storms started because they ached so much. Indeed, it was March that year before I managed to obtain a false set, which meant I had to go through the entire winter without a tooth in the top of my mouth.

Mrs Thwaites and I followed the path made in the snow by the animals and managed to get out of the dale all right. But we made rather a mistake on the way back, and we were picked up by an Army lorry and taken to West Friar House on the south side and given hot tea and something to eat. We did land home eventually but I think Mrs Thwaites's folks were understandably worried, wondering where we had got to.

There were no serious incidents in the 1947 winter, such as people losing their way and dying of cold, although a Mr Sowerby on the other side of the dale died suddenly whilst helping a neighbour. I believe he had a heart attack. Funnily enough, we had just as much peril when the thaw came, because it was so rapid that it caused flooding. People walking across what they thought was firm snow would fall through into fast running streams that hadn't even been there before. Luckily no one drowned but a few people got very wet!

Of course, water is a major problem at Low Birk Hatt because we have to go out to find it. We have never had water

Collecting water

simply by turning on a tap like most people. Our supply comes from the stream which flows about forty yards from the front door, or from the barrel which collects the rainwater from the roof. In summer it's easy, but winter does present certain difficulties. Sometimes I have to dig a path through the snow down to the stream and use a pick on the frozen stream. Often it can take a little while to melt down the pieces of ice to make drinking water. Usually I keep two buckets full of water but that's no good in winter because they are plastic and will not stand the frost. Years ago we stored water in a big cream pot but that came to grief during a hard frost and we had to resort on one occasion to a possing tub – that is a fluted tub made from galvanized metal which was common to most households before washing machines – which, of course, had to be used for soaking the dirty clothes on washing day. This was when I was a girl and we had a lot of calves to feed and water.

On occasion there isn't sufficient water available from the stream or the rainwater tub, and I have to go down to the reservoir, which I call the Mississippi, to rinse the washing. In recent times I have been able to go down to the hostel, where my good friend Richard Megson gives me the opportunity to wash in lovely hot water. But it's a fair distance to walk there and it is, I suppose, a lot handier to pop down to the reservoir. I can have the washing done and back home again by the time I get to Richard's place.

To be honest I never get much washing done during the winter months. Usually it is done during the summer, certainly for my better clothes.

As for toilet facilities, I have an earth closet so the lack of water does not affect that side of things. Trouble is, the closet does get full and I have no means of cleaning it out. It's such an unpleasant job and I just cannot cope with it. In the old days people used to put ashes on top, but I prefer to use a utensil and I take it out on to the pasture. Not a thrilling subject to discuss, but it is the most practical method.

I suppose it will be the winters that will eventually finish my deep attachment to Low Birk Hatt, now that I am getting older. Two years ago, for example, I had a rough time. The weather became very bitter up here and because it had been a bad summer I had kept two of my cattle in the byre by the house all the time. This meant I had to get hay from the top barn for the rest of my cattle, which were still outside. So I dragged the sledge two fields up to the top byre, and the going was tough because of the mole hills. And I had a slight mishap, the simplest thing in the world, really, when I was using a shovel in the calf house. I had a bullock, a nice quiet beast, called Charlie, and I lost my grip on the shovel when he knocked in to me. Unfortunately, the shaft went over the top of my foot and Charlie stood on it. It hurt a bit at the time, but I got myself free and didn't think a lot about it just then. I still had to get the hay down from the top byre to take to the cattle in the bottom byre on my sledge. Because of the pain I couldn't manage to pull the sledge in the uphill parts, so I had to break the bales in half, tie them up separately and carry them to the level bits, and load up again. It had been a very hard frost, the path was very slippery, and that night was particularly cold. My foot was giving me murder, and it got worse during the next few days, but I still had to go out and fodder the cattle. I didn't strap it up or anything like that – in fact I did nothing with it. But it healed itself eventually. All in all it's an experience I would not like to repeat.

A Bird's-eye View of Baldersdale

To appreciate properly the difference between a winter which the majority of people experience and the kind with which the people in the high Pennines have to cope, you need a bird's-eye view. It can be a revelation to fly by helicopter from the A1 at Scotch Corner, up the valley of the Tees towards the high country, when the temperatures fall and the skies become leaden. The fields around Barnard Castle can be quite green and pleasant, but a few miles further on you meet the snow line. From then on it becomes an arctic scene. Two or three miles out of Barnard Castle you can see a light covering of white – enough for pedestrians to consider galoshes but far short of a digging out job with the shovel. But at the entrance to Baldersdale, the difference is dramatic. Here the land rises to a thousand feet or more above sea level. And just over the moors in a northerly direction is Birkdale where the counties of Yorkshire, Durham and Westmorland meet by a perpetually angry stream called Maize Beck and the hills soar to a deep-frozen two thousand feet.

When a flurry of snow lightly dusts the roads and pathways of the urban and suburban areas you can be sure that Baldersdale and the rest of the high Pennines will be thigh deep. When the research for *Too Long a Winter*, the first film documentary about Hannah, was being finalized around the end of October 1972, a certain hope was expressed about the weather. It would suit the purposes of the programme if there would be snow on the ground when the film unit arrived in November. The landlord of the Fox and Hounds in Cotherstone, which stands at the entrance of Baldersdale and was to become the front line headquarters for the film makers, scoffed at this idea. He offered a complimentary bottle of wine if there was any significant snow around the pub when they arrived to commence filming in November. Came the day, and the film unit – a ponderous line of vehicles, carrying half a ton of exceedingly expensive equipment and all the people required to make it work efficiently – rumbled out of the centre of Leeds. The weather was benevolent for the time of the year. A few rain squalls perhaps, but the temperature was well above freezing.

However, there was to be a significant change as the convoy journeyed further north. At Scotch Corner, the rain had changed colour. It was white and floated around. Five miles from Cotherstone it began to blow a blizzard. By the time the film crew arrived at the door of the Fox and Hounds, the drifts were rising to eighteen inches. Not a word was spoken as they made their way to the bar, but a well chilled bottle of wine was uncorked and waiting . . .

The next two weeks will never be forgotten by all those who were privileged to work on *Too Long a Winter*. On one occasion a furious blizzard howled across a landscape illuminated by a sunset of bloodshot gold. Two men held out their sheepskin coats to shield the camera from the slanting snow, another lay full length in the drift to hold the tripod steady as Hannah led her white cow out of the storm and into the byre. It was a wondrous sequence, which would later move millions of viewers.

A few days later, the storm became so violent that sheep became buried in six-foot drifts of snow, and the camera recorded farmers scrabbling down with their hands to release buried sheep, pin-pointed by amazingly perceptive border collies. The Yorkshire Television helicopter, which had lifted the crew in, landed in pitch darkness, totally against the ground rules laid down by the Civil Aviation Authority, and lifted out the film equipment. The pilot, who was as skilled as he was courageous, wisely refused to return to lift out the crew.

It was seven miles from that location to the nearest road, where the crew vehicles were parked. The route back had been totally covered by snow. Fortunately, the crew were not then aware that in recent recorded history three men had perished trying to walk the same route in midwinter. They had simply lost their way because the track was obliterated, and had wandered in to oblivion – frozen to death. By 1972, presumably to guide people in the same predicament, posts five feet high had been driven into the ground beside the track. Along some stretches only eighteen inches were visible. But the way to safety was thus signposted. Some hours later – no one counted, but it was a long time – eight soaking, snow-covered individuals just – but only just – on the right side of hypothermia made it to the main Teesdale road, which snow ploughs had kept open. They were amazed and delighted to find on that isolated junction the tiniest pub they had ever encountered, tucked away in a bend in the empty road. Fifteen people would have packed the place out. It was totally empty, and the landlord clearly expected no custom whatsoever that evening since he was reclining in his private quarters. But he had lit a good coal fire in his bar. He probably thought it was the gale that blasted his door open, but for the next hour he was busy dispensing more whisky than he would normally expect to sell in a week. Or, perhaps, a month.

Every working moment of those two uncomfortable, exhausting, memorable weeks were lived on the extreme edge. The generator which tried to make it to Low Birk Hatt Farm, to

Hannah with Her Ladyship on the 'new road'

provide camera lights, turned over on its side and had to be hauled out by tractor. After one session filming from a helicopter the cameraman's limbs were so stiff he was 'locked' into a sitting position and had to be carried to safety and warmth. Everyone suffered from that daily and prolonged exposure to a Baldersdale winter – swollen faces and aching joints were commonplace. Everyone, that is, except Hannah. She moved with a nunlike tranquillity from one sequence to the next, thinking nothing of being asked to drag a beast through a blizzard, and clearly suffering none of the discomfort felt by others. The elements may have seemed brutal to the documentary makers (and some had roughed it in various parts of the world) but to someone like Hannah who had experienced the winters of 1947 and 1962 that November was child's play.

In between the exterior locations Hannah sat by the coal fire in her kitchen, and by the illumination cast by an oil lamp, as the camera turned, she described her incredibly spartan lifestyle. Living alone, with no electricity, no water on tap, one cow and a calf, and an income of £280 a year – 'if things go well'. Her expenditure on food for the month had edged up to £5! These provisions were left for collection by a local grocer on the dry stone wall by the single road that winds through the dale, a long and difficult walk from Low Birk Hatt.

Essentially, Hannah was a castaway of life. An only child, all her relatives and close friends in Baldersdale had either died or moved away, and she became an abandoned person in a mostly abandoned dale. It is hard to imagine anyone else in this island who was more isolated and more materially deprived. Yet no resentment showed as she talked about her life and philosophy. Nor one jot of self-pity. Indeed, she seemed well content with her lot in life, and her face shone as she outlined her thoughts. She spoke in a curiously musical, richly accented way with a certain pattern that could only be described as antique – as though the speech mannerisms of the local dales folk of two centuries ago had been preserved within Hannah. Clearly the lady could communicate. Everyone at Yorkshire Television conceded that as the film rushes were viewed, sequenced, edited and dubbed. But no one could have envisaged then with just what power.

Hannah's film was transmitted at 10.30 p.m. on Tuesday, 30 January 1973, to an audience approaching five million – a very respectable rating for a documentary shown at a time when most people are either retiring for the night or thinking about it.

The instant response was very favourable and next morning the reviews were superb. All the quality papers led with an assessment of *Too Long a Winter*, and marvelled at the astonishing life led by this old lady with the gleaming white hair in that frozen lonely Yorkshire dale. Old lady, indeed! She was only forty-six at the time, but sheer hardship and constant exposure to the worst elements the high Pennines could mete out had drained her youth away. It wasn't so much that she looked old and wrinkled (if you could discount the gleaming white halo of hair) since her complexion was as smooth and pink as an infant's. But she conveyed an impression of someone much older because her movements were restricted by rheumatism and her limbs made frail by lack of proper nourishment over the years.

On that first morning after transmission, none of the production team had the slightest idea of the impact the film – well, Hannah Hauxwell – had made on the general public. But it had started an avalanche.

The first intimation of its scope came when the producer of Yorkshire Television's daily regional current affairs programme, *Calendar*, came to complain bitterly that the task of getting that evening's show on the air had been seriously handicapped. The Yorkshire Television switchboard in Leeds with its myriad lines had been jammed all day with calls about Hannah. The London office reported a similar problem, and so did the YTV branches in Sheffield and Hull. All the other ITV companies throughout the land coped with their own flood of interest. It continued unabated for two days, and the gallant switchboard operators were near exhaustion. Fortunately, most of them had seen the programme and were committed admirers of Hannah.

Then came the mail. The GPO in Leeds rang to say it would have to make special arrangements to cope with the volume, and delivered bulging sacks direct to the production team. The general tenor of the letters, the thread that ran through the vast majority soon became clear. The correspondents expressed deep gratitude to Hannah – they were so inspired by her sublimely tranquil and uncomplaining acceptance of the kind of material deprivation considered unacceptable by modern society, so moved by her angelic demeanour and indomitable spirit, that they had been obliged to consider their own situation, and concluded that their individual complaints about life were so paltry by comparison that their entire perspective had been changed. Most enclosed a gift – 'please, please accept it Hannah – I feel I owe you such a lot' – ranging from cheques up to one hundred pounds from people one hoped could afford it, down to postal orders for fifty pence from pensioners. Cash, too, in all denominations – and then the parcels followed, clothes, food, presents of all kinds.

The Press leapt on to the story. They realized a new star had emerged and a most unusual one at that. Photographers arrived to take pictures of the mail bags, and the Yorkshire TV still of Hannah inhabited the front pages for weeks.

The stunned production team were dealing with the tidal wave as best they could when an awful realization dawned. What had they done to this woman? Completely ruined her life? A team was dispatched immediately to Baldersdale and discovered a remarkable scene. The lanes in the dale were full of people trying to locate Hannah, some in caravans. Fortunately, the isolation of Low Birk Hatt is its own security so Hannah was spared the arrival of a regiment. The few who did get through, mostly mature if determined ladies carrying packets of tea, butter and biscuits, did not create any serious inconvenience. It transpired that Hannah was well capable of coping with this sudden celebrity status, displaying a curiously ingenuous confidence as in later months she met people ranging from royalty to hard-nosed journalists, and completely disarmed them all.

Only the money pouring in by every post seriously concerned her. At first she declined to accept it, wanting it sent back. She was persuaded to concede on that point, then proposed to share everything with the production team – until it was pointed out that if just one penny, or a single biscuit was diverted in that direction, and it became known, we'd be lynched.

Hannah's film had a dramatic effect wherever it was shown, and won a clutch of awards. Gifts and visitors came from all over the English-speaking world as television stations overseas, alerted by all the publicity, snapped up transmission rights. A group from Switzerland turned up on the doorstep of Low Birk Hatt on her birthday (they knew – they had gifts), a whole cheese arrived overland from New Zealand, and the rooms at the farm began to fill up. Perhaps the most confused man in the Yorkshire Dales during the first frantic days after the first transmission was the Baldersdale postman. If anyone ever deserved a hardship bonus, it was him. The people at the GPO were also remarkably efficient, since letters addressed as vaguely as 'The Old Lady in the TV Programme, Somewhere in the Yorkshire Dales' were faithfully delivered.

It seemed that half the world wanted to give Hannah something and a classic example occurred when the programme was shown by a Dutch television station. When a senior executive arrived at the studio a day or two later he found parcels piling up in the reception area. He telephoned Yorkshire Television to seek explanations and advice, demanding plaintively in a gutteral accent: 'Who the hell is this Hannah Hauxvell?'

The complete answer to that question, one suspects, will never satisfactorily be answered. Certainly she rarely fails to surprise as she faces up serenely to various situations which would disorientate people with much more sophistication. For instance, when the Yorkshire Television helicopter landed on her doorstep for the first time, it was feared that the experience may be alarming to her, something akin to an alien spaceship settling on to the average suburban lawn. Not a bit of it. Within minutes Hannah was alongside the aircraft examining it closely, and touching it with her fingertips, as if to make sure it was real. The offer of a quick flight was accepted without a moment's hesitation and she was whisked away to join the gulls that swoop around the reservoir and over her roof. 'Now that's what I call a real bird's-eye view!' she exclaimed as she landed, beaming with delight.

There was another memorable moment a few months later when she was flown to Leeds by the same helicopter – 'I have to

Hannah opens her prodigious mail

admit, it's my favourite method of transport' – to attend a Press conference. It was her first visit to a city and she was taken aback by the volume of traffic – 'I had heard about this kind of thing, but it's quite frightening close to like this,' she said, as she stood on the pavement in City Square and watched four lanes of vehicles jousting strenuously for position. The roar of the traffic was almost drowned by a furious burst of camera shutters as the assembled Press took their first opportunity of photographing Hannah in an urban situation.

The incident which will stick for ever in the minds of those who witnessed it came when she was being ushered into the main entrance of Yorkshire Television. As she came face to face with the revolving doors her escorts stood aside to allow her to precede. But Hannah did not move, merely studied the revolving doors with interest. She showed no inclination whatsoever to go forward. Then it suddenly occurred to one of the party that these must be the first set of revolving doors Hannah had ever encountered, so he leaned forward and set them moving. 'Oh,' said Hannah, with that familiar beam; 'My goodness, what a clever idea,' and entered the building.

Many incidents of a similarly charming nature were to follow as the years went by, without any diminution in the public fascination with this spinster lady from a remote Yorkshire dale dressed in complex layers of well-laundered rags. Speaking engagements, regular television and radio appearances, countless newspaper interviews, a second major network documentary, have had no effect whatsoever on her personality and character.

She enjoys these diversions, is human enough to relish all the attention, and the material benefits were not only welcome but essential for her well-being. But diversions are all they are, and ever will be . . . not central to life. For Hannah there can only be one important base – Low Birk Hatt Farm, Baldersdale.

One day, illness, or the realization that she no longer possesses the strength to cope with the unremitting hardships of a stock farm and the 365-days-a-year toil, will force her to leave.

In the meantime, as she so sweetly says, through her tears, to those who have over many years tried to gently persuade her to go straight away and live the rest of her life in comfort: 'You are right, of course, but you see . . . I'm in chains to this place.'

4

Dreams of Romance

There are few things in the human condition more likely to create intrigue and speculation than the person who manages to progress through life without marrying, and those who have avoided a close relationship of any kind with the opposite sex arouse special interest. Hannah never married and never had a close relationship, but she had her dreams. When she was maturing into young womanhood Baldersdale was well populated with youngsters of equivalent age – that is to say eligible for Hannah. Photographs indicate that she was a bonny young lass likely to stir the emotions of any number of local young men. There was also no lack of opportunity to meet up with your contemporaries in and around the dale – there was even a dance hall of a kind.

Oh yes, it was at the Strathmore Arms at Hury, and we called it the Show Room, and sometimes the Hut. It was in the field behind the Strathmore Arms, actually. It was built of wood and it fairly shook during some of the more energetic dances, like the Lancers. The place was used for all sorts of important occasions and I can remember walking down there to celebrate King George V and Queen Mary's Silver Jubilee. I was so proud that day because it was the first time I wore a rather special red coat with matching red hat. It wasn't new of course but made of a very good material. I was also given a Jubilee mug at school, which I still have.

The first dance band at the Show Room was made up of people in the dale and they called themselves the Arcadians. Joe Donald played the drums and William and Nellie Addison who were brother and sister played violin and piano. Nellie was very good and a natural musician who could play without looking at the piano which meant she could watch the dancing at the same time. The band platform was very small and cramped, so much so that an over enthusiastic violinist could place the others at some risk from a poke in the eye from his bow.

Occasionally we would be treated to performances by visiting groups who had actually broadcast on the wireless, such as the Bainbridge Brothers, Lance and Jack, and the Swaledale Singers, who sang a varied programme of real life and beauty but created something of a problem with their final number. They chose 'In the Sweet Bye and Bye' which is a Methodist hymn and this upset a High Church person in the audience. We had our own talent in Baldersdale, of course, including a relative of mine, Norman Bayles, who had a very nice tenor voice. Whenever I hear the song 'Moonlight and Roses' I think of him because that was his favourite.

We would have visiting bands for the dances, too, and I remember one called The Five Aces who came from Copley and were very good. The favourite dances were the good old ones like the military two step, the Eva three step, the valeta and the St Bernard waltz. Not that I danced very much. In fact you could say that I was a real wallflower. You see, people tended to stay in groups, very clannish you could say, and I didn't belong to any of them. Maybe I'm being unkind, but they weren't too friendly, didn't shout out 'Haway, come on . . . thou might as well join us,' as one would have wished. They seemed to dance all the time with their own group of friends or relatives. In fact, out of all the times I went to the Show Room I was only asked to dance twice.

Then matters were made worse by Uncle's attitude. He was the man of the house, you see, since my father was dead, and he became very strict when I was around fourteen or fifteen. One night I stopped on a bit at the dance in Cotherstone and had to walk home because I couldn't get a lift from anyone. You didn't see many cars in those days and most people biked or walked. It took two hours, even using all the short cuts, to walk to Low Birk Hatt, and it was about 1 a.m. when I got back. Uncle waited up for me and was so cross that I was really frightened. So that put an end to that . . . no more dances down at Cotherstone for me.

I was very annoyed and upset at the time because there were other girls of my age in the dale and they could go and I could not. It seemed so unfair but perhaps he was right. The other girls went together in a group but I was on my own, and I suppose someone could have followed me from the dance . . . I hadn't a clue about such things in those days.

So I consequently never really learned to dance because of the limited opportunities. Mind, there was one night that I've often thought about. It was rather special, and perhaps I shouldn't mention it . . . because it was just one of those wartime things. I met him at a dance, a nice soldier who was playing double bass in the band. He had light hair, corn colour, and it was very curly. From the south of the country he was, and stationed at Cotherstone.

He asked me to dance but I said I couldn't. He wasn't put off and said that if I would please stay he would dance every dance with me. But it was something of a Cinderella situation – I had to get home early or risk another hot reception from Uncle.

It was a nice happening . . . a sweet memory. Just to think, he said he would dance *every* dance with me if only I would stay. But I never saw him again. Often I've wondered what happened to him, whether or not he survived the war. I can still hear the tune he played in the band after we talked – 'Ain't She Sweet' – and it will always remind me of him.

No, I'm afraid I've never really had what you could call a boyfriend, someone to come calling to take me out. Of course, I had my dreams, like all young girls, of a tall, dark and handsome man coming striding over the fell one day to claim me as his own. And I used to swallow up all those stories in the women's magazines, which were very kindly saved for me by two ladies down the dale. There were romantic books too, such as *A Mad Love* by Charlotte M. Graham, and *East Lynne* which I think is a great, great book. Another beautiful volume was *The Rosary* by Florence M. Barclay which is a story intertwined with a song which I heard once on a record sung by Paul Robeson. I've read lots of books, including several of the classics but haven't liked some of the authors some dote

on, like Jane Austen and the Brontës. I considered that the story of the Brontës themselves is more interesting than some of the characters and situations they wrote about. I've only read *Wuthering Heights* of theirs as it happens, and I wasn't too keen on parts of that. I thought that Heathcliffe had no redeeming features at all. I know that some ladies think it so romantic, the meeting on the moors with Heathcliffe and everything. But they are welcome to him. I wouldn't have gone to meet him under any circumstances.

Oddly enough I never met anyone I thought I might like to marry when I was younger, in my teens and early twenties. It was much later on in my thirties and on one occasion even later than that, when I met two men who at different times became very special to me. But it was just my foolishness – I am sure neither ever felt that way about me. They both retained a certain affection for me but not in the way I wanted.

It wouldn't have worked out with the first gentleman as it happens, because although he had a lovely smile, he was a ladies' man and he did like drink too much. I think he had a little corner in his heart for me but if we had got together and he had gone off with someone else I couldn't have stood the hurt and humiliation.

Anyhow he went away and met the lady who became his wife in London, I believe, and they had a child. We still remained good friends.

Now the other gentleman I liked very much. I was in my forties when I met him – call it middle-aged madness if you like – but he was so kind and thoughtful. It wasn't as though either of these men had led me to expect anything, gave me anything to hope for, it's just that I really liked them, particularly the one I encountered later on. He got married a year or two later and had a son and a daughter. Funnily enough – now this makes me think a bit, although it was probably just because he liked the name – he did call his daughter Hannah.

Oh yes! I've had my dreams, and I do feel that, if you have never had a close relationship with somebody, something in you dries up . . . goes dead, one might say. They say that machinery works better when in use. But if I had been given the chance when I was younger I might easily have made a mistake and gone for good looks and he might have turned out to be Old Nick to live with. Since getting older I've sometimes hoped for someone with whom to have a good relationship. Not to marry, but just to meet up on a regular basis and do nice things together such as walks, long discussions about books and music, that sort of thing.

There are some people who have a remarkable ability to attract the opposite sex, and sometimes it *is* sex that it's all about. But I think that sex can be a fleeting thing and sometimes I believe that if it is that alone as the basis of a relationship, then all the finer and better qualities are thrown out of the window. Personally, I do not think that sex is important, but if there is someone you like, and share affection, interest, respect and trust, then perhaps sex can mix in a little. But I put it at the bottom of the list and consider it can really be done without. And then, of course, it becomes less important as the years go by – that's one of the compensations of getting older.

On the same subject, I suppose I have to point out that I have never really wanted to have children. I have never liked babies, and I am not really comfortable with them when they get older. That is not to say that I haven't met some canny little folk, but generally I don't speak their language because I have never been used to them. I realize there are some women, and I know one or two in Baldersdale, who cannot resist babies and go all to pieces whenever they meet one, whereas I am the same with dogs. I'm just daft about dogs.

Under the circumstances then, perhaps it was wisely ordered that I never found a man to form that special relationship. But I have sometimes thought there might be a problem in the afterlife, if there is such a thing – one hopes but I am not convinced – when one is supposed to be reunited with one's loved ones. I have been to funerals in Baldersdale where bereaved people have shown supreme faith, being convinced that death is only a temporary thing and that they would meet up with their loved ones again.

So maybe I will lose out a little in the romantic sense when it comes to my turn. Of course, one hopes to meet one's parents and other dear relatives, but there won't be someone special to me.

And now it seems that I will go to my grave without meeting that special person.

5

My Music...
The Talented Tallentires
and a Poetic Grandad

Hannah's apparent simplicity and innate modesty cloaks many talents. One night during the making of the first film in November 1972, she dusted down a piece of furniture in that crowded kitchen of hers (which everyone had supposed to be a writing desk) lifted the lid and revealed . . . a miniature organ! Hannah explained that it was one of the elegant gifts that her mother had brought down when she was given in marriage to her half-cousin (on the Tallentire side of the family), William Bayles Hauxwell. The film crew gathered around to admire this splendid piece of furniture, clearly an antique of considerable interest, possibly value – if it was in good order and free of worm and rot. Did it still work? Hannah smiled, pulled out a stool (which had seen better days) and began to play. She had never mentioned that she possessed musical ability, so the crew listened spellbound for a few minutes as she played the carol 'Silent Night, Holy Night', as though she had been rehearsing for a month. In reality, she hadn't touched it in years. Instinctively her audience came out of their bemused state and worked quickly. The lights were swung round, the Nagra tape recorder switched on and the camera hastily placed on its tripod and pointed. The result was another memorable moment in *Too Long a Winter*. Still clad in her tattered working clothes, her wellingtons pumped away assiduously to give the instrument the breath it required. It turned out that Hannah had inherited a natural gift for music.

I did have a few lessons, with a lady down the dale called Annie Bayles. She lived at New Houses, and was related to me in a mixed up kind of way – her father and my grandmother were cousins, but what that made me to Miss Bayles I cannot imagine! It was the year before war broke out in 1939 and a small sum was paid for a quarter's lessons, thirteen in all, I think, but I did miss one or two. Mother was a grand player, of course . . . much better than I ever was . . . but she thought I might do better if someone else taught me, and she was such a busy person with all those old people to care for and Daddy ailing like he was.

It turned out to be a lot easier than I thought because I was scarcely quick on the uptake when it came to lessons. But I found I could just sit down and play by ear. I do not claim to be gifted – it's just something you either possess or you don't. I must say it was a great relief not to have to try to understand it all from books.

Mother would play really good music at home, and I still have her books of music – Beethoven, Chopin and Tchaikovsky. It was lovely to listen to, one of the treasured memories of my childhood in fact. But as times became more difficult with the passing years I suppose she had neither the time nor the inclination to play music.

Mother was a Tallentire and it was that side of the family which had the interest in music and . . . well, talent, I suppose, like the first part of their name. They were rather better off than most, I think, and they owned an inn called New Spittal, between Bowes and Brough, over to the west. I believe it may be the Bowes Moor Hotel now, which I hear is quite a large and important establishment and in a very good position on the main road to the M6.

They had a variety of musical instruments, including violins, and my Grandfather Tallentire created quite a stir locally in later years by travelling all the way to Manchester to hear the Brothers Hamburg play. I cannot imagine how on earth he even came to know about them because it was long before radio was introduced. Anyway they were called Mark and Jean, pronounced in the French manner. One played the

Hannah's mother as a teenager with the lady who looked after her

piano and the other the violin and they were quite celebrated. Grandfather's principal interest was to hear the one who played the piano but when he got there he was rather taken up with the violinist. He could play both instruments himself.

The entire family seemed to be steeped in music and I understand that when a new harmonium was introduced in Spittal Chapel there was keen interest in comparing that with the one they owned – such as whether one had more stops than the other.

Obviously the younger members of the family became too enthusiastic about it all because Grandfather Tallentire threatened a different kind of stop if they carried on spending so much of their time playing and talking about music. He thought, perhaps, that not enough attention was being paid to work. Indeed, he had, in fact, smashed one of their violins when he lost his temper for the same reason in the previous year.

Of course, most people around here relied on Chapel for their music, and very good it was too. The Tallentires were staunch Chapel folk even though they owned a pub. I am not sure how they reconciled that situation, since the Methodists were very much against alcoholic drink. I am not sure about the precise details, but I do believe than when Great-Grandfather Tallentire became old and decided to retire he refused to allow his sons to carry on the licence.

Anyway, the Tallentires never gave up their music because when Grandfather Tallentire set up house in a little farm called Northside he went to buy an organ but took a fancy to a piano and came back with that instead. He was the one who went to hear the Brothers Hamburg.

Mother carried on the tradition in our house and she was a talented musician. I am sorry to say that I never heard her at her best because of circumstances.

Now on the Hauxwell side, I had a grandad to whom words were music. He played a very happy part in my childhood and just the thought of him makes me smile even today. James was his name, and he had a wonderful way with a poem or a recitation, and could remember dozens of really stirring

Grandfather James and Grandmother Hauxwell

examples. He came to Baldersdale a hundred years or so ago
to help construct the Hury Reservoir – I think Low Birk Hatt
was built around the same time. He was born around the
Darlington area and I heard that his family once had money,
but lost it in some way. Mind, he was rather a wild card was
Granda, rather too fond of strong drink. He would often go
down to the Hare and Hounds at the west end of Hury – it's
gone now of course – but he was a grand man and his scarum
ways did not alter my affection for him one bit. Granda's
fondness for alcohol is one of the reasons why I have never
touched it in my life . . . although I do admit to having some
rum sauce once. But no, I do not want to take the chance
myself in case it turns out to be a family weakness.

When they were younger he and Grandma had a little farm and I think that Grandma did not have an easy life with him and had to do a good bit of the farm work. She was also a grand needle woman, a talent which rather curiously led to a change in her religious affiliations. Ever since the Wesleys brought their message into the western dales, Methodism had been the strongest religion around here and we had a nice little chapel in the dale. The Church of England hadn't a place of their own and were obliged to use a room in the school-house for their services on Sundays. The school was connected with the Church in some way, although it had been built by Dalesfolk with dales money. Anyway, the clergyman who came to look after those who were C of E got to know about Grandma's skill as a sewer and also knew that a little bit of extra money would be welcome in her household. So he arranged a job as a sewing teacher at the school for her. I suppose she was so grateful that she became one of his flock. But her daughter, my mother, stayed with the Methodists. As for me, I went to both establishments as a girl – Sunday School in the afternoon at the church and evening service at the chapel.

I must say that the Methodists had the edge when it came to music and poetry, and Granda used to encourage me to take part. Chapel Anniversary was always a treat and one year I sang a song, 'Won't You Buy My Pretty Flowers'. Then I would do a recitation, sometimes one of Granda's favourites like 'The Arab's Farewell to his Steed'. I can still remember most of the words to this day:

> My Beautiful, my Beautiful,
> that stands so meekly by
> His proudly arched and glossy neck
> and dark and fiery eye.
> Stranger hath thy bridle rein,
> thy master hath his gold. . .

And of course it all ends happily when the Arab obviously cannot bear to part with his horse:

Who said that I had given thee up.
    Who said that thou were sold
Tis false, tis false my Arab steed,
    I fling them back their gold.
Thus I leap upon thy back,
    And scour the distant plains
Away, who o'er takes us now,
    May claim thee for his pains.

Oh, how I do like those lines, and when I repeat them now it brings back so many happy memories of that scamp of a grandfather of mine.

6

Festive Times...and

Funerals

People who live, work, play and die in the more remote rural places like Baldersdale are distanced from the rest of us, and not just in the geographic sense. Their lives have a totally separate base, their vital points of reference are distinctly different from the majority who dwell in the more materially blessed urban areas. There, one is largely protected from the extremities of nature. But in the higher reaches of the Yorkshire Dales, there is nowhere to hide. The forces of nature, even today, are in control, and a winter storm which will inconvenience town and city dwellers can still devastate the hopes and aspirations and the economic structure of a Dales community. When Hannah was young and in her formative years, this dichotomy was even more pronounced. The difference is essentially one of the spirit and it manifests itself in the habits and attitudes of country folk. Stoicism replaces sentimentality, pragmatism is preferred to romance, and the need to survive from one season to the next overrides everything. Hannah Hauxwell possesses an unusual sensitivity for one who was reared to the truly spartan life of an isolated dale in the thirties and forties when sheer hardship invariably deadened any aesthetic tendencies. It was a community which was lagging behind the lowlands by at least a century. Electricity and water on tap were unattainable dreams for most, but then, nobody had much time to indulge in dreams. Every day of the week, fifty-two weeks of the year, the toil was relentless. Cows to be milked twice a day, every day, water to be carried to all the cattle, fodder to drag to the high pastures, hay to be cut if the weather was benevolent, dry stone walls to be repaired after the ravages of winter, cows to be·calved and ewes to be lambed (usually in the middle of the night), horses to harness, drains to be dug . . . the list is endless. It is truly remarkable that, given the scant time for leisure, a fine appreciation of music and literature existed in certain isolated pockets of Baldersdale which Hannah was privileged to enjoy. And Chapel was uniformly well supported because of the unswerving belief of people who live in this way that some enormous, inexplicable force shapes their destiny. The hours spent in this manner would have to be paid back, though, usually at the cost of sleep.

The women of Baldersdale, as in all similar communities, went with their men in to the fields and byres and worked shoulder to shoulder. They were excused few, if any, tasks. Hannah may appear to be a frail pensioner but a lifetime's exposure to the hard labour of rural life enables her to endure the most extreme elements far better than urban-reared people half her age.

The women, too, had to cope with all the household duties, including feeding men and hired hands with appetites honed by constant fresh air and exercise, with none of the labour-saving aids which most women took for granted. Naturally, Hannah had to take her place on the Baldersdale treadmill, working to the orders of her uncle in the fields (her father died when she was an infant) and assisting her mother in the kitchen and wash house. In some ways she was very unsuited to this life – indeed she has described herself as a 'misfit' in Baldersdale. Despite her bleak background and threadbare, Dickensian sartorial habits, she certainly transmits an aura of elegance and gentility. Her delicate mannerisms and overall maidenly demeanour suggest that she would be much better suited, say, in the tearooms of Cheltenham or Bath, with life revolving around the quieter charitable events, bridge parties and chamber music. This gives the impression that a tiny error has been made in the Grand Design.

Hannah is, for instance, sentimental about animals, not a common trait among Dalesfolk since it is counter-productive in a society geared to the continual slaughter and selling of cattle, sheep and pigs. She became aware at an early stage that there was an entirely different way of life available not far outside Baldersdale, perhaps more appealing to her, but it could have been on another planet.

Hannah clearly possesses a unique quality which gives her a remarkable perspective of the very fabric of Baldersdale. She may perhaps have felt a little out of place but she articulates a rare understanding of what was going on in the place, all underpinned by an almost total recall of the fascinating minutiae of day-to-day events. When it came to the major events in the life of that other world outside Baldersdale, such as Christmas, the celebrations were muted, to say the least.

At Low Birk Hatt we didn't have Christmases in the generally accepted sense. Mother had so much to do outside and the old folk living with us were ailing and needed a lot of attention.

Christmas dinner rather depended on the weather. If it was stormy people were too busy looking after the farm and the animals to bother much, but when it was clear we had a nice meal. Once we had a goose but Mother was so ill that she had to go to bed after she had roasted it. I was told that before she got married and gone into farming she lived with a great-aunt and enjoyed a good meal every day. A different way of life altogether.

Nor did we make much fuss over presents. Mother did once give me a tin of toffees, all wrapped in gold paper, which was a special treat – I still have the pretty tin, all pink, red and gold. I would get a stocking with a few bits of things in when I was young and Grandma used to make a big cake with white icing, but that would be when Daddy was alive. But school was a different thing at Christmas, and very nice too. We were given crêpe paper to make hats, lanterns and crackers, and Mrs Archer would provide us with a sweet or a nut to put in the cracker. Then we decorated the school ready for a really splendid children's tea in the afternoon, which was usually followed by a lantern slide show in the evening for the parents, also very enjoyable. It was always a bit dull and unwelcome coming back home to Low Birk Hatt afterwards.

Strange to say, I didn't really like carol singers. There was something rather eerie about people turning up unexpectedly around the door and starting to sing. When I was small I would creep into a corner. I suppose the best Christmases I

*Hannah at six with her
mother*

To my Dear Dad wi[...]
our Best wishes.

W.B. & L.S. Hauxw[...]

(Hannah at [...] 6, with mo[...]

knew happened over at Clove Lodge where Mr and Mrs Atkinson and the Misses Hind would always make a special thing of it. They had a juniper bush which was placed in the hub of a cart wheel covered in crêpe paper. We would decorate it with pieces of cotton wool for snow, and one or two other nice things like those shining coloured balls, which seemed to be metallic, but which were easily broken.

But Christmas at home was very quiet. We didn't invite friends with Mother being placed as she was, but if neighbours called they would be offered a glass of something, usually home-made ginger cordial, and a bit of cake if we had it. We didn't have parties, nor did we celebrate my birthday as most children do. Uncle wanted me to have a twenty-first party but 1 August is an inconvenient date because it's usually in the middle of haytiming, so we didn't bother.

One Christmas, Mother managed to find the time to make me a dolly, but only because I pestered. Maybe I was being a bit greedy because I already had the one I have mentioned before made by Mrs Fawcett from West Birk Hatt. But Mother must have known how precious dollies were to me and set about making me a black one taking the pattern from my old one, which I called Cuddles. She used an old black quilted petticoat and found some furry black fabric to use for its head and feet. Now that was a really special present.

When I look back I realize just what a hard time Mother must have had because she did not enjoy what one might describe as robust health. In fact she became ill soon after I was born. She got out of bed too early, so the story goes, because there was so much washing piling up belonging to all the family, as well as me. Anyway, Mother became very ill with pleurisy and my father had to poultice her.

We never did have a proper wash house at our place like some people, with a big boiler and a fire underneath for hot water. Nor did we have sinks and drains, so all the water had to be carried in and carried out again when it was dirty.

I still have the big iron mangle she used to wring out the clothes. We didn't even have liquid or powders then, just Sunlight soap, which Mother cut into pieces and dissolved in a large iron pan on the fire. Then it would be mixed with the hot water in a possing tub, which was made from wood in the early days, but eventually we acquired a zinc one. The clothes were agitated by hand, using a wooden dolly, which had four short legs and a long handle.

Mother did all the cooking as well, and there was a problem in that department too because our oven was going home – that is to say, it was on its last legs – even before the war. But Mother did the best she could and made rabbit pies, apple pies, and obtained a very good recipe from Mrs Fawcett for a tattie cake, which was a bit like a Cornish pasty, without the meat, and a whole lot bigger. There were cakes and custards and home-made bread and teacakes, when people brought us fresh yeast from Barnard Castle. Mother was really a good cook but that oven was not exactly reliable – indeed, I do not know how she managed to get such nice things out of it.

We had a garden where vegetables and fruit grew very well. Grandad was the gardener and planted a lot of fruit trees, including gooseberry, blackcurrant, plum and loganberry for the jam-making. We even had a walnut tree which is still going, but it does not bear fruit any more. He was also very fond of flowers, and as well as things such as marigolds, pansies, marguerites and wallflowers, he grew a rose one doesn't see these days, which was very white when it first came out and then developed a lovely flush of pink. And it had a lovely perfume. So did the Southernwood which was a feathery blue-green plant – that's another plant I've never come across since, although I have to confess that I haven't seen many gardens. Grandma would use it for her button-holes when she went to church, along with a flower or two.

I've heard say that Grandad used to rise at five o'clock in the morning during summertime to water the garden, all carried by hand, of course. He was so proud of it, and rightly so. But when Grandma died he just lost all interest in the garden, and since no one had the time to take it on, it became neglected. The nettles took over and nothing survives now.

It was such a shame because Grandad James Hauxwell had lived a life somewhat fuller and more exciting than most in Baldersdale. I understand he was always ready for a bit of mischief and they used to tell many tales about him. He had two brothers, one called Robert, who was employed in the household of the Duke and Duchess of Northumberland as a footman, I believe, and another called Frank who became a policeman. They were both very smart and correct, but Grandad was a little more wayward. He joined the Army – twice! First time his parents bought him out, but then he went and signed on again. He went down country with the Army, and there's a big difference between there and up here – it's not a place where economy is considered in the same way, so maybe he learned some bad habits, such as a tendency to alcoholic drink. Of course he acquired some better habits, such as that great liking for poetry and music.

Grandmother Hauxwell and Uncle Thomas Tallentire Hauxwell who lived with Hannah

Anyhow he came back to farming after leaving the Army. When he was young he used to live in a place called Manfield, near Darlington, along with his brother. Incidentally, the one who worked as a footman had to leave his job in order to get married to a girl who was also in service at the Duke's place. Apparently matrimony was not permitted for the servants.

Grandad went to work for a farmer who was rather an old skinflint. Another young man was in service there too, but he was from a rather well-to-do family who had paid the old man to teach their son the tricks of the trade. But he was granted no special treatment and had to toil just as hard as the hired hands. In fact, the farmer was so mean to this young man he determined to exact revenge. So when threshing time came round he bought a considerable amount of liquor which he concealed in strategic places.

Well, before mid-afternoon all the men – and extra help always came in for the threshing – were incapable of working. I daresay that Grandad enjoyed that because there is no doubt that he was fond of a drink. He could get up to all sorts of tricks and I was told that when another one of the lads at the same farm applied for a job as a coachman, Grandad gave him a reference. He had a lovely hand, and wrote about him that 'this man has been my coachman for a number of years and I have no hesitation in highly recommending him . . .'. Goodness knows how he signed himself, but I do believe it worked, and the lad got the job.

Grandad arrived in Baldersdale around the turn of the century, to work on the building of the reservoir, and came to lodge at Low Birk Hatt, when Great-Grandfather Tallentire was running it. It seems that other young men came to stay too – I suppose it must have been a very welcome extra source of income – and I understand that Great-Grandmother Tallentire was criticized for allowing young men to stay in the house when she had daughters. I do believe that came about because of an incident for which Grandfather Hauxwell was responsible. You see, Great-Aunt Jane was a skilled dressmaker and made clothes for quite a number of young ladies in Baldersdale, and it was usual for them to try on the new clothes and have the final fittings in the kitchen. It seems that Grandfather either found, or perhaps made, a hole in the floorboards. And I'm afraid the young men used to use it as a peephole whilst the young ladies were in a state of undress. Eventually they were found out, and you can just imagine what a fuss that caused, all those years ago when Victoria was on the throne, and even the sight of a petticoat was forbidden to young men.

Yes, Grandad was something of a harum-scarum but I loved him nevertheless. I think his experience of farming was somewhat limited because of the time he had spent in the Army, and that would not make things easy for Grandma

PEACE
PERFECT
PEACE

May there be no moaning of the bar,
When I put out to sea.
Tennyson

In Affectionate Remembrance

OF

WILLIAM BAYLES,

Beloved Husband of Lydia Sayer Hauxwell,

of Low Birk Hatt, Baldersdale,

Born *April 15th, 1896;*

Died *January 29th, 1933.*

Interred at Romaldkirk Cemetery on Thursday,
February 2nd, at 2 p.m.,
Cortege leaving Residence at 12-30 p.m.

"Thou shalt be missed; because thy seat will be
empty."—*I. Samuel xx.*, 18.

"AT REST."

"Suffer little children to come unto me and
forbid them not, for of such is the Kingdom of
Heaven."

Now I have reached that happy place
And am forever blessed,
Now I see my father's face
And in his bosom rest.

In Loving Remembrance of

THOMAS ISAAC,

THE BELOVED SON OF

Richard and Elizabeth Tallentire,

Of Lowfields, Stainmore,

Who died on the 13th of Feb., 1892,

AGED 4 YEARS,

And was Interred at Brough on
Wednesday, February 17th.

Some funeral cards

Hauxwell because she had to take on more responsibility around the farm. Perhaps because of his liking for drink, Grandmother would have to be the overseer, and do a good bit of the work herself. But Grandad did have certain very useful talents. He was particularly skilled with animals and he knew something about veterinary work which came in very handy when any of the animals took ill, also during lambing and calving time. Horses were his speciality, and although he was rather a stout and shortish man – he sported a moustache – he was quite strong.

The passing years took their toll, of course, and he did go into a decline when Grandmother died. Because of the unusually large number of old folk living at Low Birk Hatt we had more than our share of funerals and everything was made worse when Daddy died at such a young age. He was only thirty-six and I was too young to remember much about it. He started with pleurisy which turned into pneumonia and because he wasn't a strong man it carried him off. I used to sleep in the same bed as my mother and father because of the shortage of space, but one morning I woke up in another room and I looked out and saw the undertaker standing at the top of the stairs.

Funerals are very special occasions in the Dales, when people who may not be on the friendliest of terms would forget their differences for a while and come and pay their respects. Most everybody turned out, whoever it was. There was a custom called bidding, when the family of the deceased person would have cards printed to send round the dale. The relatives never delivered the cards themselves, but would choose a group of friends or neighbours. Some would take them to the top half of the dale, and the others the bottom half. In that way people were bidden to the funeral. The post would only be used for people who lived out of the dale. I still have all the cards to this day.

I was only a little girl when I went to my first funeral. Grandmother Hauxwell took me when her brother, John Bayles, died. Mind, I stayed at the house and didn't have to go to the graveside, but I can still see the procession of people.

95

Some came on foot, and others on horseback, or horse and trap. The coffin was carried on a horse-drawn cart because it was a long time before a motor hearse became available. Most people wore black and those who couldn't afford dark clothing managed to borrow some, and the men wore hard hats.

Daddy went to his grave at Romaldkirk in the same way, on our cart which was pulled by his favourite horse, a little cob called Dick. On occasion, so many people turned up to a Baldersdale funeral and the church or chapel became so crowded that people had to stand outside. I recall having to stand out in the cold at Cotherstone Chapel when one gentleman belonging to a family which had been in the dale for several generations was laid to rest. He was from the south side of the dale, which by custom went to Cotherstone, whilst we on our side went to Romaldkirk. There is no burial ground in Baldersdale itself.

I do not remember much about my father – just odd memories, like when he would lift me up on his horse and give me a ride. And when he would arrive from Barnard Castle with a heavy load of shopping on a bicycle and give me a nice round bun he would buy as a special treat from a shop called Guy's. He was a very serious man, I'm told, and totally unlike my uncle, his brother, who came to live with us and run the farm when father died. Grandma used to say they were like chalk and cheese, and that they should have been shaken up together in a bag to get more of a mixture. Then both might have been more sensible. Uncle was much more the happy-go-lucky extrovert whereas Daddy was shy and reserved, but that may have been due in part, at least, to the burdens he carried. He worked all hours, day and night, and in all weathers. I do know that at Low Birk Hatt, after finishing working in the fields all day, he would set to joinering at night, and made several of the doors and gates. I daresay he might have appeared more cheerful if his responsibilities had not been so heavy. You see, quite apart from all the work, he had such financial problems, particularly with the large mortgage on the farm.

Hannah and friends

Hannah, Barry Cockcroft and tape recorder

Hannah and some of her belongings

OPPOSITE ABOVE: *Hannah's kitchen window – view slightly impeded*

OPPOSITE BELOW: *Hannah asleep in her four poster bed*

ABOVE: *Winter in Baldersdale*
BELOW: *Feeding the cattle*

At the door of Low Birk Hatt

Mostafa Hammuri
1982

ABOVE: *Low Birk Hatt; Barry Cockcroft (in sheepskin jacket)*
BELOW: *Hannah with her dog Timmy*

ABOVE: *Hannah with Ashley Jackson, celebrated Yorkshire artist*

BELOW: *Ashley Jackson's view of Low Birk Hatt*

Hannah's father as a young man

With Uncle's help we all struggled on after he died, and when I got a bit older and left school it was not possible for me to contemplate leaving home to find a job and a new life outside Baldersdale. I was needed at Low Birk Hatt. You see, Mother was very subject to bad colds and influenza, even when she was young. She was no giver-in, but sometimes she got very high temperatures and just had to stay in bed. As for Uncle, he had suffered from rheumatism for as long as I can remember, so, all-in-all, we always had more work than we could really cope with. So I didn't have the same opportunities as other young people in the post-war years.

The very worst time came when Mother really took ill. The doctor sent her to hospital where she stayed some time, and had X-ray examinations, and I was so worried. But they didn't find anything wrong, so Mother came back home, and I was so happy. I'm afraid that desirable state did not last very long. That bad epidemic of Asian flu arrived and all of us caught it,

Hannah's mother as a young woman

Mother, me and Uncle. Unfortunately, Mother, who was sixty-seven, never really recovered, gradually became worse, and early the next year the doctor said she must go back into hospital for more examinations. Before that could be arranged she took very poorly one day and an ambulance had to be sent for – luckily one of the nearby farms had a telephone. But all the local ambulances were busy and we had to wait for one to come from Richmond, which is many miles away. She died before the ambulance arrived at the hospital. I didn't go in the ambulance because there was the cattle work and all the arrangements to do, but a good neighbour, Mrs Britton, from High Birk Hatt, was with Mother.

A terrible blow it was. One of the worst things of my life. If Uncle hadn't been there to support me I do not know what would have become of me.

They brought Mother back to the chapel, which is disused these days. She didn't come back to Low Birk Hatt. But before the service the hearse drove to what we call the Hill's Gate – that's the gate from our land to the main road.

So in that way Mother bade farewell to Low Birk Hatt. It was Uncle's idea, and a very good one. What a dreadful day that was, and I was on my own because Uncle had to go away to attend to business matters. They don't stop even for funerals.

Mrs Britton very kindly put on a tea afterwards and Mrs Fawcett, that grand person from the old days, was very comforting. But you could say that I have never really stopped missing Mother. She was such a heroine in her own way because it was not possible to give her the attention and comfort she deserved yet she never complained. I will never be the woman she was.

Uncle survived Mother by three years, and those were not easy times. He was older, seventy, and his legs began to give him such pain. I did my best, but it became more and more difficult to do the work on the farm and look after him. He had difficulty sleeping and sometimes would call out in the night for me to help him light his pipe. Towards the end he could no longer fend for himself and good neighbours used to come and help me get him up out of bed and into a chair. But then we had a spell of bad weather during haytiming, a difficult situation at the best of times, and I simply could not manage. Uncle had been in bed for about a month by then, so the doctor arranged for him to go into hospital in Barnard Castle.

He never came back. Again through the help of kind neighbours I was able to visit him now and again, though not as often as one would have wished. One day the hospital rang Mrs Britton to say he had died, and to pass on the news to me. She even very kindly offered to attend to things, but I would not let her do that because I knew I had to face up to my responsibilities. So I went myself to see the undertaker, select the bearers, and arrange all the funeral details. It was a wintry day when Uncle was buried, with a bit of snow around. The service was held at the chapel and everyone went to the Kirk Inn at Romaldkirk afterwards. It wasn't the custom, really, but the landlord and his wife, Mr and Mrs Wallace, were friends of the Brittons' and knew Uncle as well, so they agreed to lay on a nice tea.

There were no flowers. That wasn't a feature of funerals in Baldersdale and our family never had flowers, not even for Mother. We believed that flowers were for the living, and Uncle used to often quote some lines of poetry:

> The flowers you are going to bring to my funeral
> Bring them now, for I want to see them.
> The kind words you have to say about me,
> Say them now for I want to hear them.

I decided to have a farm sale after Uncle went, and put up all the livestock for auction. There were about fifteen cattle, around a dozen sheep and a few lambs left over from the spring lambing. But I chose the wrong time when prices were depressed and there wasn't a great deal to come after all the expenses were paid. Apparently, if I had waited a bit longer prices would have been much higher. But then I was never much of a businesswoman and I had no close relatives left to turn to for help and advice.

I was all alone.

100

7

My Friends, the Beasts of the Field

❧

Life for Hannah Hauxwell then settled into a pattern which basically continues to this day. She kept one cow which each year produced one calf to send to market. The income from that sale, plus a little rent for pastures rented out to other farmers, produced a pitiful income which, when the first documentary presented Hannah to an amazed public in 1973, was running at about £5.50p a week.

Out of that she had to pay all expenses, including animal feed and coal, which left around five pounds a month for food. No running water, no electricity, and she couldn't even afford to keep a dog. After the transmission of the film, which conferred instant celebrity status, the economic situation improved dramatically, and she invested in more cattle to boost her income. But she had for several years been living a life which the word frugal does not even begin to describe accurately. And it was all compounded by a feeling not just of loneliness but more a sense of abandonment, as all the families she had known since childhood began to leave Baldersdale. And she was an only child.

It was to her animals that Hannah turned for companionship – even conversation! She lavished upon them the sort of affection she would have given to her family had there been any. They all had names. When Hannah made her first public bow, she was constantly in the company of an elderly white cow called Her Ladyship and her love for this awkward beast touched a certain public soft spot – the British are well known for their protective, caring attitude toward animals. The media are aware of this fact, and photographs of Hannah side by side with Her Ladyship featured in a hundred newspapers and more.

Well, Her Ladyship was rather special because she was with me for many years and supported me by producing calves for market. Not that I ever took them myself, because auction rings are a bit rough and noisy – places for men, really – so a kind neighbour would attend to things for me, such as arranging transport and attending the sale. I would just wait at home and hope for the best – you know, that a decent price would be bid. It was rather an important event for me in those days, as you can imagine. Just having one calf a year to sell instead of a sizeable number like most farmers.

Fourteen years we were together, Her Ladyship and me. I do not suppose most farmers would hang on that long. Inevitably she got down, and the day came when she had to go, for her own sake really. Frank Bainbridge, the same man who took the calves to market, once again organized the necessary procedure. Another man came and he was canny, too – didn't make things worse. I didn't stay to see it happen, just went as far up the fields as I could go. I know these things are inevitable but . . .

These days I have Rosa, a daughter of Her Ladyship. She is fourteen and a half, and still in pretty good shape. There have been lots of others, of course, and I remember a lovely beast called Daisy who would have been grand. But nothing happened when I had her served so she had to go. Then there was The Bumpkin, and Septimus – I was particularly sorry to lose them. Nowadays I have three breeding cows, including Rosa, who is the senior beast. There's Patch, because she has a patch, and she has a daughter, Bunty. Then I have Puddles, sometimes called Bumble, because she is daft and somewhat nervous. I still have to carry water to her because sometimes she won't come out of the byre and follow her mother, which means that she is left all on her own. One feels sorry for the little ones in some circumstances and they nearly become like children – but not quite. But I have to admit I become very attached to them and I know it's a fault.

When I was a child we had two bay-coloured horses, and I later got to know them very well. Dick and Snip they were called, and Daddy was quite attached to Dick. He was only

Hannah with Her Ladyship

small, but a very willing little man even though he suffered an accident when he was young. I recall the time when Daddy had been very ill with pernicious anaemia and had to stay indoors for quite a while. Well, the first time he came out of the door when he was a little better, he shouted for Dick, who was in the top pasture. And Dick came galloping down to greet

Sweeping hay at New Homes, Baldersdale, 1938 (Beamish)

him – it was quite something. I used to ride both horses in the early days to take them to be shod over to Lowson's Smithy at Romaldkirk. Later on we took them to Woody Swinbank's at Mickleton, but that's been turned into a pub now, appropriately called the Blacksmith's Arms.

When I got a bit older I worked with the horses in the fields, particularly at haytiming. Snip, the mare, wasn't as friendly or cooperative as Dick, and used to be very awkward when I was

sweeping the hay with her. Once the sweeping machinery fell over and I sprained my wrist.

Uncle brought his own horse when he took over at Low Birk Hatt, an old grey mare called Madge. She had a foal one year, and Uncle thought a lot of her. One night he was over the moors around North Stainmore and had to return home at dead of night. There wasn't a light anywhere, but Uncle just gave Madge her head and she brought him safely home. But she got too old eventually and so did Dick and Snip, so we had to send them away.

Then we bought a lovely horse called Prince with much better breeding than the others. He possessed a lovely long tail which swept right down to the ground and it was a lovely sight to see him turn round. Uncle was always wanting to have that tail cut shorter and we had quite a few battles about it, but I won and Prince kept his long tail. Because of his fine pedigree he was a little bit more highly strung than the others and would set off rather sharply. He had no really bad faults but you had to be careful that nothing startled him, such as a bird suddenly rising, and on one occasion he did bolt. Once I had a rather nerve-racking experience with him when I was working the horse rake in the lower field.

I got into a mess with the reins when I was turning and Prince began to reverse towards the edge of the ghyll by the side of the field, which had a sharp drop. I couldn't stop him and I was so frightened that horse, machine and me were going over that I jumped off. But I kept hold of the reins and Prince just stopped in time. I still dream about Prince.

In later years we borrowed Blossom, a big Clydesdale-type mare, from John Sayer at West New Houses, and eventually we bought her. But she had a strange temperament and we were told by one man who worked for John Sayer and had helped to break her in that she wasn't right in the head. She had a foal with us during the dreadful winter of 1947, and her behaviour became even worse, so much so that our good neighbour Mr Britton said she wasn't fit for a young woman like me to work with and insisted I borrow his horse Bobby, a very even-tempered animal.

Hannah with Blossom

The last horse we ever had was the best, a plump little Dales pony called Thomas. He didn't just eat to live that horse, he lived to eat, which was obvious when you saw how fat he was. But he was the most pleasant animal to work with. Some horses become excited and upset if something goes a bit wrong when they are in harness, such as chains or ropes becoming entangled around their feet. They will often rear or kick out and generally create a real commotion. But Thomas never bothered, just let you get on quietly with sorting out any mess like that. As long as you fed him plenty, he would be most cooperative.

Over the years I have done all kinds of work with horses, hay-making, spreading and harrowing manure and hauling coal down from the road on a sledge. Hay-making meant long days and tough work, all by hand. At one time we would have to hire a man in for a month, eating with us but sleeping in the barn. Everything depended on the weather and if your luck was out the hired man's time could be up and not much hay in. I still remember the names of some of the men we hired over the years – there was Billy Lockie, Mark Dent, and an Irishman called John Boyne.

Childhood memories are always best, of course, and everything was so much better when my father was alive. In those days we would always start the hay-making at Hury, a parcel of land we owned two miles down the road. It had a house which once had a thatched roof, but it had gone derelict and a tree had started growing in the middle of it. Just the three of us, my parents and me, would go down to Hury and stay there for two or three weeks, or until the work was done. We left the older ones in the family to look after Low Birk Hatt, do the milking and other chores, and we went down with the horses. We must have made quite a sight trailing along the road with scythes, rakes, forks, the sledge and the sweep, mowing machine, and our food in a basket. And a bed! The house still had a good warm loft, so we all used to sleep there. Oh, I did love our times together at Hury, with Mother cooking supper over the fire in an old iron grate and the nights so romantic and balmy. There were lots of wild roses and foxgloves growing around the lanes and fields and you could smell the hawthorn and rowan tree blossom. Those summer nights at Hury will stay with me for ever. Everything comes to life in the summer with the long days, the moon to illuminate the darkness, and the birds calling to each other in the trees. My parents used to sit and talk about going to live there permanently one day! I know they loved the place and Daddy planned to mend and restore it for us. But that dream went when he died.

Apart from hay-making, the other important events in Baldersdale, or any other farming dale, centred around the animals, and we kept the usual selection. After the cattle, the sheep were economically the most important, followed by the pigs, hens and geese.

Lambing time could be quite hectic since we had about sixty sheep at one time, and a good crop of healthy lambs to be sent

Sheep dipping at West Birk Hatt. Left to right: Sam Fawcett; Tom Fawcett, Sam's bachelor brother; George Fawcett; and Hannah's uncle Thomas Hauxwell

Sheep shearing in Baldersdale

109

to market was essential. We also had to shear and dip them every year and friends would come to help. The Fawcetts had a sheep dip and we would take ours there, but the shearing was quite a problem for me. Uncle used to tie the legs of the poor beast and then I could get a fleece off, but it was a method expert shearers used to scorn. Trouble was, I just couldn't hold the sheep properly – but then I have to admit I never liked doing it. It wasn't the sheep, it was that greasy wool that caused the trouble. I liked the sheep well enough, particularly when they were lambs. Sometimes when the little ones were weakly or had been abandoned by their mothers, we would have to take them inside and feed them by hand.

Our wool used to go to a firm called Ackroyds down in the textile area of the West Riding of Yorkshire, but years before the war a gentleman called Watson Taylor would visit the dale. He was a representative of a mill called Waddells and he had a strange-looking horse-drawn vehicle, square shaped with high sides. He used to take some wool, but mainly he was there to sell and his cart carried samples. He had some lovely tartan coloured rugs which I used to go and admire over at Clove Lodge, where he would take lodgings for the night. People would give him fleeces to take away to be finished off, perhaps coloured, at his mill. I know Mother traded with him from time to time, and once sent a quantity of wool away to another mill and had some back as grey blankets. But they weren't the same superior quality as those Mr Watson Taylor brought because they wore out. The tartan rugs from Waddells would still be going today I imagine. I haven't seen the like in many years.

Both Grandma and Mother were clever with their hands, making mats and quilts. Grandma laboured for years with her frames and turned out all the mats for the house. I have still got two quilts that she made, which have been in use for as long as I can recall. Mother knitted a white cotton quilt before she married, which I treasure to this day. I have done a bit myself, but possess neither the ability nor the patience to do fine work. I prefer thick wool which gets done rather more quickly, and during the war I unravelled some of Grandma's things and knitted them up again. In those days we had to use an oil wool, which was all right after you washed it, if somewhat coarse. I knitted myself a dress from that which started off fawn, but we ran out of that colour and I had to finish it off in blue. Maybe it wasn't the last word in smartness – far from it – but it was very warm and comfortable, if rather too big. I made a scarf and then set off to knit socks, but got into a mess with the difficult parts and Mother finished them off. The last thing I knitted was a red pullover for Uncle which I have yet. But I was never as good as Grandma who produced lovely crochet work with intricate floral designs. My work tends to be more durable than artistic.

Of course it was nice to know that some of our things were made from the wool from our own sheep. I had my favourites, of course, particularly one which I called Nanny Bateson. It came to me as a gift, a little black-faced lamb sent to me by the Batesons who were farming Briscoe at the time. She grew up into a grand ewe and produced a lot of lambs for us. I had other pet lambs, but Nanny Bateson was the first and the best-remembered.

We sent the lambs to be sold at auction in the autumn. A little man called Maurice Tarn was the auctioneer, and the sale was held in the fields alongside the Strathmore Arms. Other income came from the calves we had to spare and everyone would lose quite a bit of sleep when the cows were calving since the event would invariably happen in the middle of the night and it was often necessary to play midwife in case of complications. Losing a lamb or two was not unusual, but a dead calf was a serious matter.

I didn't care much for the hens and geese but I had quite a high opinion of the pigs. Most people think that pigs are dirty and ignorant, but I had many happy times with them. They let me look after and feed two piglets when I was a little girl and they were really friendly and affectionate. I used to play with them for hours on end and they tore a big hole in the back of my coat during one rough and tumble. I didn't give them names, which was just as well because they both had to go to be killed.

Later on a neighbour sold us a reckling – that's the runt of the litter, too small to be really valuable – and I did name him. Joss grew up into a very pleasant pig, and some can be very temperamental and even nasty, and he stayed with us whilst Mother was alive. Then I'm sorry to say he made a bacon pig.

I have known some pigs which were really rather clean. It helps if you keep the place tidy and regularly mucked out, and we did have one which kept its bed and its toilet place quite separate. Oddly enough our pigs didn't do so well at market. To us they were lovely looking animals, but, would you credit it, they said they were too fat!

Pig killing was quite an event in the dale and had to take place when there was an 'R' in the month because it was wise to avoid the warmer months since refrigerators were unknown in the dale. And because one would share with neighbours, it was rather spaced out so that people could benefit over a longer period.

I used to avoid being present at the killings. When I was a child they killed one close by me and I heard the squealing. So always after that I would make sure I had a job to do as far away as possible from the scene, because it upset me a lot. I made my escape you would say, and I know it was the coward's way out, because I have to confess that I thoroughly enjoyed the proceeds.

For some years a man used to come in and do the deed, but Uncle got on with it himself later round by the stable, using a humane killer. Then the throat would be cut to drain off the blood to make into black puddings – I wasn't too good with the blood either, but it was tasty afterwards.

The pig would be hung up on a big strong hook and there was much to-ing and fro-ing with kettles of boiling water to help scrape off the bristles and extract the entrails. Nothing was wasted. The liver was usually eaten first and some of the tasty bits, like the spare ribs, sausages and chines – that's pieces of the backbone – would be sent round to friends and neighbours.

The kitchen then became a hive of industry, with the fat being cut up and rendered for lard, kept in a big earthenware pot. Brawn would be made from the trotters and the ears, and then there was the head. I never had a lot to do with the pig's head, but it did make lovely potted meat. It all took a lot of hot water and big pans.

The flitches – that's the hams – were laid down in salt and saltpetre to cure, then hung up on hooks. Mother used to put a bit of sugar on as well. I cannot understand why our pigs were criticized for being too fat because the meat was so sweet and tender, almost like chicken.

I always helped with the sausages. Uncle used to do a bit because he liked fiddling with machines, and the one we had in the early days was borrowed and not really suitable. It was a big machine which I think had not been set up right – it seemed to have more blades than necessary. But Uncle liked to play around with it. Mother and I were much happier when we acquired our own machine and we could get on with it together. Those sausages were a credit to Mother because she knew just the seasoning they required, and we would hang them up in the kitchen for people to eat as they pleased. One would stand on a chair and cut a piece off at mealtimes. I preferred them when they were fresh because they had a bit of a tang later on, but they were so good that the thought of them makes me hungry.

8

Housekeeping...and Health

Public exposure on television and the continual attention of the rest of the media did have a marked effect on Hannah Hauxwell. She insists that it was entirely benign. And, remarkably, it changed her personality not one whit. She preserved her dignity, independence and way of life. What it did do was confer material benefits, which were desperately needed at Low Birk Hatt. The threat of malnutrition receded and vanished forever, and the twentieth century finally arrived with a team from the North Eastern Electricity Board. However, there are still serious problems.

It all started when a man called Frank Somers wrote to me and enclosed a photograph of himself and his wife Pauline and their little girl called Hayley. A very nice letter it was too, but just one of many from people who had seen me on television. Indeed it was difficult to cope with all the letters in the early days after the first programme.

Then he turned up and explained his ideas about bringing electricity to Low Birk Hatt. It seemed to be an impossible dream at first because of the distance and the difficulties. And, of course, the cost – that ran into thousands. But he was so moved by the film that he launched a campaign to raise the money at the place where he worked. That was called Lancro Chemicals, a rather large firm in Eccles, near Manchester. He managed to borrow a copy of the film and showed it in the works canteen and raised most of the money. Yorkshire Television made good the shortfall and the Electricity Board set to work. Those poor men had a lot of problems driving in the poles to carry the lines and were obliged to use explosives

Hannah watches workmen bringing electricity to Low Birk Hatt

on the last stretch over my land because they came across solid rock. Then Frank arrived one weekend with a team of his workmates to wire the place up and install the plugs and light fittings. We had a grand switch-on with cameras from Yorkshire Television recording the moment for their regional

115

magazine programme, *Calendar*, and all the newspapers covered it, too. A lady from Doncaster wrote and offered me a cooker, so Frank and his friends went to pick it up, overhaul it and bring it here. That, and the electric kettle, given to me by a good friend, are a great blessing.

Someone also presented me with an electric washer but I have never been able to use it because there isn't water in the house and I wouldn't be able to understand it anyway. But after the second programme Yorkshire Television installed block heaters throughout the house in lieu of a fee, so Low Birk Hatt was heated properly for the very first time. It was just as well because the back boiler in the kitchen split in two about fifteen years ago and I haven't been able to light a fire in the grate since.

Until then I had done my cooking, such as it was, on that fire. Things were not very good in those days, and the financial situation was very worrying. There was no great amount of money coming in and one was continually minding the pennies. The food bill had risen to five pounds a month and, with being so tired with all the work, I suppose I neglected myself. I lost some weight and felt ill enough to go to the doctor who sent me to hospital in Northallerton. Altogether I was away from Low Birk Hatt for two months and those kind neighbours of mine came to the rescue once again and looked after the animals.

I must say that I enjoyed my time in hospital. I made a lot of friends and was introduced to the wonders of television for the first time.

Nowadays I am a lot better placed and able to eat better because of the electric cooker. I tend to have a lot of sausage and bacon because it's easier and my time is somewhat at a premium with around a dozen cattle to care for. But occasionally I will take the big pan and fill it with onions, carrots and potatoes for a grand stew. Washing up is a problem because of the business of having to fetch water and heat it up, so I do not bother much with tinned soup, which can make pans such a mess. And I don't stand the cans in hot water in case it marks the bottom of the pan and spoils it.

Hannah snatches a meal between tasks

As you might imagine my monthly food bill has gone up quite appreciably, far more than the five pounds a month just before the programme *Too Long a Winter* was made. When you count in a bag of calf cake and the general groceries, including the eggs, it will come to more than thirty pounds these days.

That will include the meat for the dog and brown bread for the cat. I prefer white bread myself, because it makes better toast, but I always get a brown sliced for the cat which likes a little bit of butter with it.

Being able to afford a dog now is another advantage. I have had one or two in recent years, mostly given to me by kind

117

people, but things didn't work out with them. But now I have Timmy, a nice little man and a grand companion. When I fall asleep in my chair he always sits on my lap. He's a Jack Russell so I'm hoping he might do something about the rodent problem at Low Birk Hatt. All farms have rats and mice but in recent years they have been coming through from the barn into the house and getting into the furniture. I'm afraid I have to suspend my perishables, like bread, cheese, butter and vegetables, from the ceiling in plastic bags or they would get at them.

I know the rats are a worry because they are so dangerous and can contaminate food. Last winter I came face to face with one on the landing – I don't know which of us was the more scared. After that I made a habit of sending Timmy upstairs ahead of me when it's time to go to bed.

Now I am very well aware that a number of good friends worry a lot about my situation and my health, particularly in the winter, but I manage quite nicely, thank you. I know people imagined I was much older than I was when they saw the first film because some newspapers referred to me as 'the Old Lady of the Dales'. But I was forty-six at the time! Now I am a pensioner, rising sixty-three, and some people say I have changed very little. Of course, I do have a few problems, but I have good caring doctors who have prescribed medication.

For the last two years I have had to take two tablets a day. It's for what the doctor calls angina. Such a nuisance it is because it's a condition which makes you tire more easily, leaving you short of energy and breath. It can be very annoying when you are wanting to hurry, chasing the cattle up a hill or something. I also have some other tablets, smaller ones, which I have to take if I get a pain across the chest and it persists . . . what I call a chuntering thing. There can be this dreadful tired feeling with it, too, which is very frustrating when you know time's getting on and you know you cannot delay the work any longer. I will take two in that sort of situation. Otherwise I seldom touch them. I think it better for you if you can avoid things like that, although I have no authority for saying so. I do understand that some people with my condition have to take goodness knows how many tablets of one sort or another each and every day, so I suppose I am fortunate.

My eyes are another problem. I was a little foolish in earlier years before the electric light, trying to read and sew by the light of an oil lamp and pressing on when I should have stopped and rested my eyes. It must be ten years since I went to the optician and I keep promising myself I will go when the opportunity presents itself, because I love to read. In the days when I had more time to spare I would read any book I could lay my hands on and particularly enjoyed anything about foreign lands.

I am often asked what if I had an accident or I collapsed and there was no one around to help. But there is an arrangement to cater for an ·emergency of that kind. The two local policemen came around one day and suggested I place a red light in a window which could be seen by as many neighbours or passers-by as possible. I was to switch it on if in serious trouble. Richard Megson, who runs the hostel over at Blackton, very kindly came over to fix it up for me. I do hope and pray that I will never have the need to use it.

Travel...

From Tommy's Bus

to the Savoy and

Buckingham Palace

Until she was approaching her half century Hannah was probably the least travelled person anywhere in the northern counties. Yet, paradoxically, in another way she has more experience than most. On several occasions visitors to Low Birk Hatt, in the middle of discussing their planned holiday or business trips abroad, were startled by Hannah's detailed knowledge of the places they were due to visit. Especially if they happened to be Paris, Venice or Florence. Hannah read extensively about the classic cities when her eyes permitted such luxuries and still absorbs information from radio and television like a sponge. She has a fine appreciation of art, literature, music and architecture, and clearly a thirst for travel.

I have often thought how interesting and useful it would be to have a globe in the house. Then one could spin it round when news, travel or holiday programmes on radio and television specify certain places and you could see where they were in relation to Britain and the rest of the world. Marvellous as a map is, a globe gives you a far clearer idea of the overall situation, with the world being round.

Mind you, travel was very much an academic thing for me until the television programme and even now I can scarcely say I am a travelled person. These days everyone seems to be hopping on and off jets if only to go to the Spanish holiday resorts, but I have never left these shores. Indeed, the furthest I had ever been in my pre-television life was a day trip to Loch Lomond on a bus. Before the war, a man called Tommy Oliver ran a bus service for the people of Baldersdale. Now there was a pleasant, outgoing and jolly man, and I am glad to say he had a long and happy life. Tommy's bus was the very first form of public transport that I encountered because he came every Wednesday to the head of the dale to take us to Barnard Castle.

The bus held about twenty people, but it carried all manner of other things. I have seen poultry and rabbits and large baskets of butter and eggs sharing seats down to Barnard Castle. I think the fare in later years was half a crown return, and he would park up near the Post Office, so that people could come and leave their shopping with him instead of humping it about the streets. The return journey was supposed to start at half past three but there would always be a few people missing. But Tommy was so good natured about everything and he would sally forth and start asking people where his strays might be. Sometimes the bus didn't set off until nearly four o'clock. One day Tommy had to let someone else drive and that man set off at three-thirty prompt. That caused some consternation and I don't think the same person deputized again.

Tommy did all the pre-war Chapel outings. I had my first glimpse of the sea on a Sunday School outing to Redcar when I was about ten. I couldn't swim, never have been able to, and I didn't go out on a boat because along with the rest of the family I have always been afraid of water. The sole exception was Mother – she liked riding in a boat and went out with her close friend Mrs Fawcett, who took her boys along, too.

The last trip on Tommy's bus was to the Lake District. Then he and his wife retired to take on the Post Office at Romald-kirk, some time before the outbreak of war. He delivered the letters and ran a little bit of a farm he owned, whilst his wife looked after the Post Office. The Oliver family was long established in Romaldkirk and they had a shop selling meal

and other products. Tommy was one of a number of boys, and he also had one sister.

After the war a man called Alec Howson in Barnard Castle ran the trips and it was with him that we went to Loch Lomond. Now that was a feat of ability, patience and sheer physical endurance. We left Clove Lodge at six o'clock in the morning and arrived back at four o'clock the following morning. Alec drove all the way, with breaks of course, and it was a marvellous experience.

We went with Alec for quite a few years, and sometimes Mother would come too. She was with me on one occasion

when we went to Saltburn where they had some Italian gardens which I liked very much. It was there that I first heard 'The Skater's Waltz'. I couldn't work out whether it was a band playing it or a record but that tune will always be associated with the trip to Saltburn.

Of course, we have our own local beauty spot, High Force, which is a spectacular waterfall further up Teesdale. I have only ever been there once with a family related to me; I suppose they are my second cousins, Norman and Lizzie Bayles, who farmed at Stoop Hill, a small place just outside of Mickleton. Norman Bayles was a cousin to my father and was related to Mother through the Tallentire family. Although the family ties were not very close, we have always been very friendly and spent quite a lot of time together. It was usual for us to call when we took the horses over to Mickleton to be shod. Mother and Uncle would come as well and we had some lovely times together, full of music and laughter. Music was very important to Norman and occasionally he would come over and invite me to concerts and films. Once, Reginald Forte, the famous organist, came to Middleton in Teesdale and I had the pleasure of attending that concert. Norman and Lizzie had two daughters. Marjorie, the youngest, was a schoolgirl in those days. Lizzie used to lend me books which I looked forward to getting. We would go to Middleton Carnival with them when time and circumstances permitted, and one lovely June day we went to High Force and had a picnic. We sat on a tree that had been felled and ate some very tasty ham

Harvest Home at Lartington Hall

sandwiches –one of the few picnics I have ever been to. Of course, my horizons broadened considerably after the documentary. First of all I was invited to lunch in Leeds and they sent the helicopter for me, piloted by Captain John Leeson, who had done all the flying for the aerial shots in the film. I had been his guest in the air very briefly before when I was taken up to see Low Birk Hatt as a bird would see it, and I

Lartington Hall (Northern Echo)

125

found it a thrilling experience, quite the best way to travel. Leeds was the first city I had ever visited and when I was taken by car to the television studios I had my first encounter with revolving doors, which I found rather strange. I'm not very good with things like that. I met some very interesting people, including Fred Trueman. Now I knew he was connected with sport but I didn't know whether it was cricket or football. So I had to ask him to make sure, and he was very nice about it. I really enjoyed our conversation.

I went back home by taxi because it was too dark for the helicopter to fly, and I'm afraid I do not travel as well by road. But some tablets were kindly provided and they did alleviate the problem. However, I had a funny reaction when the taxi arrived back in Baldersdale – my legs went and I could hardly walk. But the Atkinsons at Clove Lodge looked after me, gave me a cup of tea and saw me safely home.

From the travel point of view things carried on a bit from there in a local sense. I was invited to open functions in various parts of the Yorkshire Dales and quite a surprising number of people turned up. I had also had a very enjoyable weekend in Sheffield when the Salvation Army invited me to make an appearance. People would send cars up that rough track to Low Birk Hatt to make sure I travelled in style. I made a lot of new friends, some of whom are still in touch.

I was also astounded at the amount of mail that arrived – too much really, because I just could not deal properly with it all and I was worried in case people thought me impolite. But one day in 1977 a rather special envelope arrived, bearing an engraved card inviting me to be a guest of honour at the Women of the Year lunch at the Savoy Hotel in London. Now I know it was a great honour but I could see no way of accepting, so I put it on the mantelpiece and more or less prepared to forget all about it. However, one of my many visitors saw it and told Barry Cockcroft, the gentleman who produced and directed my film for Yorkshire Television. Next thing I knew he was at the door, insisting that I accept the invitation and asking me if I was prepared to make another documentary with him! He was preparing a series of six documentaries with the overall title of *Once in a Lifetime* and said the situation regarding the Women of the Year lunch fitted in perfectly.

He offered to make all the arrangements, such as organize the travel and someone to look after the cattle for me, so I agreed. After all I had never been to London and it is one's capital city! Barry called the film *Hannah Goes to Town*.

Well, it was all a big thrill. We filmed on the train to London and I was told at one stage that we were proceeding at one hundred miles an hour. It did not seem possible.

When we arrived at King's Cross I was told for the sake of reality I must find my own way to the Savoy Hotel, although the film crew would be close by in case of emergency. They filmed everything, of course. I had a bit of trouble on the Underground with all those automatic machines but one of the station staff spotted that I was in difficulty and came to my aid. I negotiated my way to Piccadilly –those illuminations are a splendid sight – and after a few more adventures finally arrived at the Savoy.

Well, the place was just a dream . . . completely out of this world. I was escorted to the fifth floor and shown in to a riverside suite which was named after Sir Charles Chaplin, because he always used to stay there when he visited London. I had an enormous bedroom, and a separate sitting room and bathroom. The wardrobe was unbelievable, you could walk in at one door and out of the other, several yards away. I was told that Sir Noël Coward also stayed in the same suite quite regularly.

There was a very long and comfortable settee in front of the window which had a view of the River Thames which mesmerized me to such an extent that I could scarcely tear myself away to go to bed. There were so many lights, and all sorts of colours, too. I saw ships and all manner of boats, and I was surprised by all the greenery just below the window. I thought how nice it would be to just stroll across the road and look at the river, and it appears to be quite simple until you get there and meet I don't know how many lanes of traffic.

If anyone ever gets the opportunity to stay at the Savoy,

then my advice is – take it! Apart from the temperature in my suite being a little too high for someone used to Low Birk Hatt, the entire experience was truly a once-in-a-lifetime thing. When it was time to leave and I was waiting for the car to take me back to the station for the journey back, I have to confess that I shed a tear or two.

But there were so many wonderful moments in between. We had dinner and a floor show, when part of the floor rose up as if by magic and a cabaret was presented. The next day was the big event and I wore a nice new dress in blue and fawn which I bought from Shepherd's in Barnard Castle.

Well, it was absolute chaos when I went down to the Press reception before the Women of the Year lunch. They swamped me with their cameras, tape recorders and note-books. Not that I'm complaining because I realized they had a job to do, but they were all firing their questions at once, and I do like to give a civil, considered reply. Anyway, I did some radio interviews and I was quite taken aback when I found myself over the front page of the *Evening Standard*. I cannot imagine what they were all thinking about.

Afterwards, Lady Mary Wilson, Sir Harold's wife, came and had a chat. She said she had seen the programme and wondered if it had spoiled anything for me, but I was able to reassure her that it had improved my life. She seemed very reassured. Then I was asked to join the small group selected to meet the Royal personage in attendance, the Duchess of Gloucester. We had quite a conversation. I said that I understood she came from the Continent, and she told me that she was born in Denmark. I asked if she liked living in this country. She was so nice, and later wrote me a letter in her own hand, which is a treasured possession.

Later I had the honour and privilege of meeting Odette Churchill, the heroine of the French Resistance, someone I had admired for years, ever since reading about her exploits when she received her medal after the war. She had seen the film, too, and I received a letter some time later from her husband, Mr Hallows, telling me that Odette was not in the best of health and they were moving house. So I met three very special ladies that day, and talked to a number of other nice people.

The lunch itself was held in a huge room and there was a constant babble of noise. I am not quite sure who it was I sat next to because I am such a slow eater that I did not have much time for conversation. I am not able to eat and talk at the same time, so I apologized to my neighbours for this.

The Duchess of Gloucester and the sailing lady, Clare Francis, were among the speakers, and there was an interruption when some people staged a demonstration. I thought it was in support of the IRA but it could have been some other organization, such as the Women's Liberation people. Anyway it didn't spoil anything, and the whole event will be a vivid memory for ever.

Before leaving London I saw the sights, from the Tower to Trafalgar Square and I also had a wander through Soho which I remember not so much for its more dubious side but for all the stalls of fruit and vegetables, every type, colour and description. I went into Fortnum and Mason and then across the road to speak to a gentleman dressed in very fine livery and top hat who stood at the entrance to Burlington Arcade. I also saw the statue of Sir Winston Churchill outside the Houses of Parliament and the monument to Edith Cavell; I have a book about her life.

One or two people in the streets talked to me, including the man who sold the corn to feed the pigeons in Trafalgar Square – in fact he even gave me a kiss. But my other impression of London was that it could be a very lonely place if you were there on your own without friends or relations. Everybody seemed to be rushing around looking straight ahead. People don't seem to look at other people, whereas in the towns and villages in the north that I have known the locals will bid you good day or smile as you go in and out of shops or even just crossing the street.

I really think, although I would not be prepared to put it to the test, that you could go out in the streets of London in your nightdress and nobody would notice. Of course, that might suit me because I could wear my old rags and not attract attention. I rather pity the young who live in London because they must be having a particularly difficult time.

Of course, I was insulated from the more unpleasant aspects of city life, wallowing in the luxury of the Savoy, being waited on hand and foot. All that beautiful silver and the linen, which was fresh every time, and the staff were so friendly. I had a most interesting conversation about Italian opera with a waiter called Giovanni, who was as enthusiastic as me about Verdi.

Naturally, I went to see Buckingham Palace, not dreaming on that occasion that I would not only see it again but actually enter the premises. I was invited a year or so later to the Royal Garden Party held in honour of the Queen Mother's eightieth birthday, so there I was off again to London with a film crew in attendance. I bought another dress in Barnard Castle made from very fine material with a flared skirt, and the *Daily Mail* kindly presented me with a broad-brimmed floral hat and a pair of white gloves to take some very nice photographs. That hat has been to Buckingham Palace twice because I lent it to a friend who was invited to a later garden party.

When I arrived at the Palace gates with my invitation card I was somewhat taken aback when two or three in the crowd around the railings recognized me and asked for autographs – in that place of all places! I did not know what to do or where to go, so I approached a very nice policeman, told him I was from the country and asked which gate I should use. He explained everything to me and I went across a big courtyard, through a door into a large hall, then up some stairs and along a landing turning left towards an outside terrace down to the lawns at the rear of the Palace.

Although it was July, the weather was rather cold and blustery and some people had wisely brought their raincoats, but not me! I was advised by a friend that it wouldn't be quite the thing to go in raincoat and wellies! Hundreds of people were there and I only saw the Queen at the beginning when she came out with Prince Philip and the Queen Mother and stood at the head of the terrace whilst a band played the National Anthem.

A hat for the Royal Garden Party

Some gentlemen dressed in grey whom I took to be equerries had organized us so that the royal party had two corridors, flanked by people, to walk down. I'm afraid they came down the steps and chose the path leading away from me, so I only saw those three at a distance. Several people were presented and it would have been nice to have been closer. Not that I had any wish to be presented – I mean there is all this protocol and etiquette to be observed and I may have blundered.

I was there on my own, because the Yorkshire Television film crew had been positioned on the roof of the Palace, and would have been quite at a loss but a lady from the *Yorkshire Post* spotted me and kindly accompanied me for a little while. She pointed out different people, including Prince Andrew, who was standing quite close by talking to a group of people. I wouldn't have known who it was but for her courtesy. She also fetched me tea and refreshment from one of the marquees. I enjoyed bread and butter, little flat pancakes and a nice light fruit cake. I avoided the chocolate cake because I thought it looked a little sickly.

Then I plucked up the courage to start moving around on my own and began walking down a path when the gentleman in grey asked people to stand aside, and I stepped well back. Along came Prince Charles and Princess Anne. My main impression was that they both had very fair hair and small features, which surprised me because their photographs in the newspapers give a different impression, particularly in the case of Prince Charles. Up to then I thought he had dark hair. Princess Anne smiled at me as she went by, or perhaps it was just my imagination. I wish I had summoned up the nerve to smile back.

After it was all over there was another strange and thrilling event when a car whisked me to the *News at Ten* studios where I was interviewed by someone in Leeds. It was most peculiar sitting there among all the cameras wearing an earphone and talking to someone more than two hundred miles away.

That wonderful day ended on a most romantic note when I was taken to a lovely dinner in a large hotel, still wearing my floral dress. A very gallant gentleman at the next table came over and for no particular reason, kissed my hand!

10

The True Daughter of Balder... From Another Point of View

Since it was undisputedly colonized by the Vikings, it is reasonable to assume that Baldersdale experienced a long and vivid history. So it is hardly surprising that the place has bred a line of hardy, taciturn beings who, accumstomed from birth to fighting the elements simply to survive, are not given to public demonstrations of any kind of emotion. It would probably take an earthquake or an overnight plunge in the market value of Swaledale sheep (or both) to raise the communal eyebrow. Indeed, in the last two decades there has been only one event of sufficient gravity to create stunned, almost disbelieving debate among past and present Baldersdale folk – Hannah Hauxwell, herself.

One day she was poor little Hannah from up Birk Hatt, struggling on her own since her folk died, the shy, quiet lass destined for a life of continued obscurity. The next, she was Hannah Hauxwell, international celebrity. Suddenly, their sleepy dale was full of people carrying parcels and speaking many strange tongues, all clamouring to be advised of the whereabouts of Hannah Hauxwell. The general astonishment lingers to this day.

It could have led to a certain amount of resentment, particularly when the material benefits flowed in for Hannah. Fortunately, it is in the nature of these people to be supportive, particularly towards their own. And Hannah, whatever happens, will always be one of their own. When Baldersdalians talk about her these days it is with an undiminished affection. There is a shared pride for the fame and attention she has brought to the dale. It is illuminating to listen to their own experiences of life in this isolated corner and their memories of Hannah and the rest of the Hauxwells, since it adds depth and substance to the seasons of Hannah's own life.

The Norsemen who battled their way into the northern uplands (one of their leaders rejoiced in the name of Erik Bloodaxe) must have been almost as poetic as they were bloodthirsty. They gave such lyrical names to almost every place they seized, thus perpetuating their memory for ever. When they marched into Hannah's birthplace they elected to commemorate their god Balder, which has some curious significance for Hannah's life.

Balder was a son of the most senior god, Odin, and one version of the legend says he was blessed with the gift of immunity from harm. However, it was not total since, oddly, mistletoe would be the death of him. As long as he could avoid this seasonal parasite, he would live forever. But it got him in the end. The blind god, Hod, enraged by the false words of the evil Loki, hurled a bunch of the stuff at him and Balder fell lifeless to the ground. Even then he could have been saved, so the story goes, if the giantess Thokk had agreed to shed life-giving tears for him, but for unspecified reasons she refused.

There is general agreement that Balder was not exactly a dynamic deity – indeed, he has been described as 'a passive, suffering figure'. When you consider the life of Hannah Hauxwell, and the privations she has quietly suffered for most of her life, it is reasonable to describe her as a true daughter of Balder.

'Sweet . . . shy . . . sad' . . . the same words are echoed when you speak of Hannah to those who lived and farmed alongside her over the years. One went so far as to describe her life as 'tragic'. They all, without exception, point to the harsh circumstances of the Hauxwells, which would have crushed less resilient souls. Whereas all the other farmsteads had either lusty young sons to work the land and tend the animals to improve

134

their living standards, or were able to afford to hire in permanent labour, the Hauxwells were supporting four elderly relatives at one stage, had no sons (Hannah was an only child) and were finally dealt a cruel blow when Hannah's father became mortally ill.

Their immediate neighbours helped the Hauxwells with a willingness which speaks volumes for the selfless, caring attitude common among Dalesfolk. Crisis invariably brings out the best in rural people and Baldersdale, when the occasion demanded, could act like one large family. Time and again, sons or hired hands were sent vaulting over the dry stone walls to Low Birk Hatt when it became obvious that the Hauxwells were on the point of dropping with exhaustion as they struggled to finish their haymaking or sheep shearing. Hannah herself is quick to acknowledge this magnanimity.

William Bayles Hauxwell fought mightily to keep pace with the ceaseless tide of farmwork at a time when mechanization and all the labour-saving devices now taken for granted in agriculture were but a distant dream in Baldersdale. The memory of his unremitting burden and the courageous way he tackled it is still fresh in the minds of his old neighbours and friends.

John Thwaites, one of the sons at High Birk Hatt, just up the pasture from the Hauxwells, now in his early seventies and living a happy retirement with his wife, Marie, in a cottage near Lartington, a short distance from Baldersdale, vividly recalls the painful life of William as he tilled the eighty sparse acres of his farm.

'Aye, but he were a nice fellow. And what a worker . . . he worked every hour that God sent to try and keep on top of that place. He was very like Hannah in his attitude and manner – very genteel – and I've noticed that as she grows older she looks more and more like him. Most other people says she resembles her mother, so maybe she's a good mix. Now Hannah's mother was a lady . . . a real, proper lady was Lydia. Everyone agreed on that.

'But what a tragic family they were. Every other farm in the dale was blessed with children able to share the work but all they had was elderly folk who did their level best to help but were just too old and infirm. The sad thing is that William's

John Thwaites and his bride Marie

anaemia could have been mended now. But then there was nothing they could do for him. He took cold, developed pneumonia and that was the end of him.

'I was only young at the time, but I can still recall the funeral, and the flat cart with his coffin being pulled up the field by his horse. My mother helped to cater for the funeral tea, which were community affairs with everyone helping.

'There were a few deaths in the dale which wouldn't have happened in later years. My own brother, Leonard, died from Bright's disease – that's a kidney complaint but I think they call it by a different name these days. Nowadays they have those machines to keep people alive and well.'

Trained medical assistance was hard to come by in Baldersdale during the childhood of Hannah. John Thwaites describes how the Dalesfolk, as in most other situations, organized themselves to cope with the deficiency. There were unpaid, unqualified 'nurses', usually senior ladies of the dale who possessed all the medical folklore and herbal remedies handed down from generation to generation. They were prepared to sit by the bedsides of sick neighbours to relieve the burden of their families and allow them to save their energy to cope with the farmwork. There were also recognized 'midwives' who would attend confinements and run matters efficiently until the doctor arrived – and quite often when he didn't (or couldn't, because of distance or foul weather).

There is no doubt that in times of trouble Baldersdale was a very united place – but there were, nevertheless, some curious divisions. Full membership of the 'family' was not automatic just because you lived there. John Thwaites, born in the dale in 1917, was very much aware of certain subtleties.

'My family were interlopers, and we always knew it. It didn't matter that I was born in Baldersdale, my father wasn't. He was a Swaledale man who arrived in 1910 and that made all the difference. I was never considered a true Baldersdale man.

'My father used to tell a story that shows what I mean. One day, soon after he arrived in the dale he had reason to go to another farm and overheard a conversation between two old ladies. They were lamenting that it was a sad day because outsiders

John Thwaites with Luther and Ruben Tunstace

Leonard and Madge Thwaites

were coming into the dale and taking over farms, and wasn't it a shame they couldn't be let to locals.'

The Thwaites family farmed West Hury, which had a previous existence as the Hare and Hounds public house, but left after ten years to move to High Birk Hatt in 1920. They raised three sons (reduced to two when Leonard died) and two daughters. Life, as John recalls it, was happy if hard, with not much time left over for fun after the daily toil was complete and certainly nothing to spare for luxuries. In Baldersdale, as in all societies, there was a definite upper strata, a small group of families which occasionally demonstrated their comparative affluence.

'Oh yes, the dale had its élite. The Dents were definitely the leaders with the Wallers, the Sayers and the Coulthards close behind. The Dents owned the very first car in Baldersdale and that created quite a stir. I remember being at school when they first drove it round the place and the teacher brought us all out on to the road to have a closer look at this amazing thing. I do not recall what kind it was, but I know that the next car to come into the dale was a bull-nosed Morris and that was owned by the Wallers.

'I cannot recall the dates but it must have been in the very late twenties if I was still at school, because I left just as soon as I could when I made up fourteen. Everybody did in those days. Discipline was very severe at that school, with the cane for the boys and the strap for the girls an everyday thing. There was one teacher who used to get so mad that she would throw slates around, with the whole class ducking out of the way. But that teacher also turned out a lot of good scholars – some even passed the examination for grammar school, although not all those who did actually went. My sister, Violet, was one she coached to that standard but she wasn't able to take her place at grammar school because the uniform she had to have was beyond the means of my family.

'Trouble with that school was the monotony. There was no variety at all – you knew exactly what you would be doing at any given moment of the week. Prayers first thing, then arithmetic, then geography and so on. There were no facilities for sport and we never played football or cricket. Physical training was done

The Coulthards of Gill House. Left to right: Henry Coulthard; Annie (daughter); Mrs Coulthard; Stanley (son)

in clogs and boots. I couldn't wait to be fourteen and be free of the place. But then I found out just how hard life could really be. I left school one day and was out in the fields muckspreading the next. And it was a seven-day-a-week job from then on.

'But when the young folk of the dale were given a few hours off we certainly made the most of it. There were dances in the Hut by the Strathmore Arms and when we grew up a bit and thought our fathers wouldn't find out we would nip into the Strathmore Arms for a pint, on the few occasions we could afford. It was pretty flat stuff, but we knew no better at the time. Not that you met girls at the Strathmore. It was strictly for males and I do not recall ever seeing a woman in there. She would have been considered trash, the lowest of the low, if one had dared to enter.'

Courtship in Baldersdale had well-defined rules. Romance between the children of established families and hired hands was firmly banned. The inheritance factor was the reason. Marriages were not exactly arranged, but the daughter of a landowning family was expected to wed the son of a family of similar means. The system caused many a broken heart over the generations. The Thwaites obviously did not subscribe to this tradition (after all, they were not even considered Baldersdalians!) since John met his future bride when she was fifteen and in service at a farm in Lunedale. Contrary to the norm for a Yorkshire dale, the young men did venture outside to seek their partners and John met Marie at a fair. Their courtship was conducted as avidly as time and finances would allow. In common with other heads of families in Baldersdale, John's father wasn't over generous with either.

'I got two shillings from my Dad every Saturday night – that was my week's wages. And I was allowed to go out most weekends. I had a bike and could pedal down to Middleton in Teesdale, meet Marie, take her to the pictures – not the best seats, mind – then buy us both fish and chips and still have change out of that two bob. As it happens, she was much better off than me because her weekly wage was five shillings.

'But there were occasions when it just wasn't possible to get time off to meet her, especially during vital periods such as haymaking. And there was no way of getting a message out to say I couldn't get out, so she would be left hanging about waiting hopefully. But she understood, because she had been brought up on a farm.

'Haytiming, we worked every daylight hour and often into the night. Every blade of grass was needed and we cut everything and anything –dykes, gutters, roadsides, hedgerows, anywhere it grew. One year I had worked nearly a month flat out, every day without a waking hour to myself. Another Saturday came round with no prospect of a night off when it began to rain in the afternoon. Me and my dad were about to cut these dykes when it came on hard. My father stopped, looked at me for a bit and then said that in the circumstances I could go out that night – providing I milked the cows first. All twenty-five of them, and all by hand, of course. By gum, cows have never been milked so fast, never. But it was still ten o'clock before I could get down to meet Marie. And she was still there, waiting for me!'

According to John and Marie, who finally married him and came to Baldersdale when she was twenty, Hannah played no part in the courtship rituals of Baldersdale. Beyond a few exceedingly brief encounters at dances attended by soldiers stationed around Barnard Castle, she apparently never had a romantic association. There is evidence to suggest that young swains showed interest from time to time but were probably defeated by lack of time and opportunity on the one hand and by Hannah's shy, reserved nature on the other. Her expectations, fed by the romantic figures of literature, were possibly too high and, sadly, Baldersdale was seriously deficient in heroes of the classic mould. But the community did have a couple of heroes in the military sense when the Second World War came, both members of a family which plays a leading role in the modern legends of Baldersdale – the Fawcetts of West Birk Hatt.

Sam Fawcett, who is warmly remembered by Hannah, was by any standards a remarkable man and the head of a remarkable family. Sam sired eight children. At least two of them were big men in every sense of the word. George and Sidney Fawcett were both well over six feet in height, both joined the regular army before war broke out, and both were guardsmen. George joined the Grenadiers and Sidney the Coldstreams. Both saw action of the most extreme kind and both were captured by the Germans. Both escaped from captivity, but only George survived.

To this day, George Fawcett is an imposing man both in stature and personality and lives in a cottage at Hunderthwaite, the entrance to Baldersdale. He has a wry sense of humour and an uncompromising disposition, particularly when it comes to talking about deeds of valour. Basically, he avoids discussion of his amazing wartime adventures, preferring to indicate that it was all a mistake.

'I didn't want to go into the Army at all,' he will tell you. 'I wanted to go into the Royal Air Force, always did. I wanted to fly – still do. If you got me a microplane right now I would get into it and fly it. I've never been in one but I've read so much about how to do it I'm sure I could manage it.'

And you believe him. George Fawcett may be in his seventies but the will is obviously as strong as ever. To learn about the story of his exploits in enemy territory it is necessary to dig out the cuttings of newspapers printed forty-five years ago. They

indicate that the big lad from West Birk Hatt is probably one of the finest unsung heroes of the last war.

The details beggar belief. George kicked off his war by joining the small group of fighting men who courageously volunteered to stay behind and fight a rearguard action in Dieppe in September 1940. He survived but was inevitably

George Fawcett, extreme right

captured. Two days of forced marching without food towards a prisoner-of-war camp was too much for this free spirit from Baldersdale and he escaped. He was on the run for forty-three days, sheltering for part of the time in a cornfield, being fed occasionally by sympathetic French farmers, but was hunted down and sent to captivity in Belgium.

They did not keep him long, however, and this time he made off with a companion and even had the nerve to work for three months on a French farm before starting a marathon trek across the entire length of France. He and his fellow escapee had been told that if they could get to Marseilles, then in unoccupied France, they stood a good chance of finding a ship bound for England. They swam rivers to avoid heavily guarded bridges and doubtless George used the fieldcraft taught to him by his father Sam to live off the land. They finally reached Marseilles, an enormous distance, particularly when you consider the devious route they must have taken, but were unlucky enough to be spotted by the Vichy French, who were in league with the Nazis. They were led in chains through the streets and dispatched to Italy. George fretted away a whole year there until the Allies landed in Sicily. He was sent in a cattle truck through the Brenner Pass to Austria where food was so short that he exchanged a piano accordian (the Fawcetts, it seems, were always able to find the means to make music) for two loaves of bread baked from chestnuts. The next year was spent in forced labour in Silesia until the advancing Russian armies precipitated another move, this one the worst of all. George was placed towards the end of a gigantic column, headed by five thousand Jews in poor physical condition. They were marched, often in sub-zero temperatures, through Germany to Czechoslovakia. The Jews fell in their hundreds and were seen lying dead by the roadside by George and the others as they passed by. He endured six weeks of this ordeal before the chance came to escape once again. The route passed through a wood and George was off like a Baldersdale-bred hare. They never caught him again. He came across a cave where three hundred partisans were quartered and fought side by side with them until the end of the war. On one occasion he played an active role in destroying a

146

German column which yielded twenty-five trucks and three tanks to the partisans. He finished up fighting with the Czech resistance in Prague until the Russians arrived. George went across to introduce himself to the Red Army, an event which boggles the imagination. They, no doubt confused beyond belief, gratefully passed him on to the Americans.

George's long war ended on a high note, partially satisfying his keen urge to fly by winging homewards with the Royal Air Force in the belly of a Lancaster bomber.

Baldersdale was *en fête*, or as near to it as the dale ever came, when Guardsman George Fawcett arrived back somewhat unexpectedly, from the war. They threw a party in his honour in the old Hut by the Strathmore Arms, where the revels were halted for one minute's silence in memory of George's brother, Guardsman Sidney Fawcett. About his brother, George will talk . . . and with justifiable pride.

'He was a regular soldier like me, went to the Middle East in 1937 and never came back. He fought with the Eighth Army and was mentioned in dispatches when he shot down a German plane with a machine-gun he had captured from an Italian plane. He mounted it on his vehicle and made it work. Then he was captured at Tobruk and sent to a prisoner-of-war camp in Italy, which was guarded by Germans. But he didn't like being imprisoned any more than me and one night made off across the wire with a pal of his, disposing of a sentry along the way. Trouble was, Sidney decided to go back to get the sentry's rifle, obviously thinking it might come in useful. On the way back again to rejoin his mate he inadvertently walked over some gravel, and the noise alerted the guards. They challenged him and he made a run for it. He was shot in the back.

'They left his body lying where it fell for three days, as a warning to the other prisoners. Then some lads from the Cameron Highlanders were given permission to bury him. He is now lying in a military cemetery near Florence.'

The Fawcetts were a fighting family, although neither George nor Sidney received a medal for valour between them – a clear injustice. Their younger brother, Geoffrey, also distinguished himself, rising to the rank of top sergeant and commanding a tank. And he survived. But there was no military tradition in the family, and despite the fame and glory won by his sons, they were still dwarfed by their father, Sam.

He must have been the best-known and most celebrated inhabitant of Baldersdale – excepting Hannah Hauxwell, of course – within living memory. Hannah herself beams with delight at the mention of his name and there cannot be a past or present resident of the dale who does not become animated when the name of Sam Fawcett is mentioned in conversation. Everyone has a story to tell about him.

Sam was a complete countryman, with a pronounced affinity with nature in all its forms. In a sense, he could charm the birds from the trees, because he adopted and tamed a variety of wildlife. His musical ability – and he was entirely self-taught – enlivened the dale for many a year and even reached the ears of the outside world when he was talent-spotted by the BBC. In 1935 he travelled to Newcastle to spin yarns and perform his music on a popular radio show of the day, an achievement equivalent to an appearance these days on a network television show. Apparently this one and only brush with city life impressed him not at all. It seems he was totally bewildered by the streams of traffic and all the noise and was very glad to get back to rural tranquillity.

Sam's other major talent was, to be frank, on the wrong side of a particular, somewhat dubious aspect of the law. Others would share the view of many countrymen, that Sam and his family were merely taking a reasonable share of what the fells and waters surrounding their home offered them. But tiresome authority deems that tickling a trout or two or felling the odd wild duck for the supper table is illegal. Poaching, in fact. And Sam was an exceedingly generous man who would frequently furnish the tables of his neighbours, including the Hauxwells, when they were ill or down on their luck.

His son, Guardsman George, freely admits that the Fawcetts helped themselves judiciously to the region's edible game.

'We couldn't help ourselves. It was bred in us. And we meant no harm, and did none. But you can be sure that no rabbit died of old age in Baldersdale during our time! My father was so good

Guardsman Sidney Fawcett, right
BELOW: *Cross marking Sidney Fawcett's grave in Florence*

with his gun that even in the dark he could bring 'em down. Unfortunately, that led to a minor accident involving the property of the Hauxwells which I suspect even Hannah will not know about. Her Great-Uncle Isaac, who lived at Low Birk Hatt, used to keep geese and one night just as the light had faded my dad shot what he thought was a duck flying off Hury Reservoir. But when he went to pick it up he was horrified to discover it was one of Isaac's geese. He decided to say nothing and quietly placed the bird by the gate leading to the Hauxwell's place, with its head tucked in as though asleep.

'They must have found it, because it was gone the day after – probably straight into the oven because it was obvious it had been killed, not just died. But to this day they don't know how.'

The activities of the Fawcett family created much frustration among the local constabulary. They knew only too well what was going on in Baldersdale but Sam and his brood were too wily to be caught and the law could expect no help from other residents. There is one classic tale, still retold with immense delight by older Baldersdalians, about the time a police constable arrived in the dale in hot pursuit of the Fawcetts. A report had been received by his inspector that a discreet cull of the wild ducks on Hury Reservoir was under way. Unwisely, he was heard to proclaim that this time he was sure to catch the Fawcetts redhanded (or, more accurately, up to their fetlocks in feathers). This news was swiftly conveyed to Sam at West Birk Hatt, who decided he would have some fun. Two of his sons were sent down to the reservoir, one at either end. When they spotted the constable stealthily approaching one end, the son at the other would fire his gun. Hury is a very long reservoir. When the perspiring policeman had raced to the spot in full expectation of an arrest, he found no trace of dead ducks or guilty Fawcetts. And as he poked around the undergrowth for hidden poachers, another shot would ring out from the far end of the water. Reinvigorated, he would set off in pursuit . . .

This sport went on for hours, well into the evening. Eventually, exhaustion forced the unfortunate man to abandon the chase. As he departed Baldersdale he was heard to announce with some emphasis that if his superiors were so anxious to catch the phantom poachers of Baldersdale, in future they could (expletive deleted) well do it themselves. He would have no further part in it. The dale rocked with mirth for days as the story went the rounds and will probably be retold for another generation to come. There is no record of any further attempts to hunt the Fawcetts.

The elder Hauxwells themselves were known to join forces with Sam in occasionally exploiting the resources of Hury Reservoir. Hannah's much loved grandfather, James, the Indian Army veteran with a love of poetry, and Sam developed an unusual method of catching eels. When a sheep died or was slaughtered, they would sometimes pack the entrails into a hessian sack and lower it into the beck leading out of the reservoir just below the Hauxwell property. After a while, the sack would be writhing with eels attracted by the delicacies inside.

Along with the Thwaites at High Birk Hatt the Fawcetts kept a neighbourly eye on the Hauxwells when they were at their most vulnerable. There was a standing arrangement: if no smoke was rising from the chimney of Low Birk Hatt by eleven o'clock in the morning the Fawcetts should come to investigate. One day the fire remained unlit because every member of the Hauxwell family was stricken with flu and unable to move. One of Sam's daughters knocked at the front door until a key landed at her feet, dropped painfully from a bedroom window. She let herself in and ministered to their needs, brewing a pot of tea and lighting a good fire.

Such generosity of spirit, added to their many talents, made the Fawcett family the most popular in Baldersdale. Everyone benefited from knowing them so a spot of poaching was not held against them. Anyway, it was not done for profit. Those were hungry days, and the Fawcetts shared the spoils. Nor would Sam Fawcett have ever upset the balance of nature in the dale because he was a naturalist and a conservationist by inclination. He had a deep knowledge of the habits of all the local wildlife and an uncanny knack of befriending them. He had a tame magpie which, in keeping with tradition, would occasionally steal shiny objects, and a short-eared brown owl which was

Stegman, Sam Fawcett's swan

quartered in his barn and developed a habit of flying at the heads of visitors and knocking off their hats. The most famous and best loved of all Sam's wild pets was a swan which he found one day lying prostrate by the side of Hury Reservoir, too weak even to stand. He carried it home and patiently set about restoring it to full health, hand feeding it for days. The swan became so attached to Sam that it stayed for twelve years. He named it Stegman (a steg is a male goose) and it spent most of the summer on the reservoir but always wintered at West Birk Hatt. It would knock on the door with its beak when it required feeding. In the end it was found mortally wounded near the reservoir, apparently the loser of an argument with a bunch of domestic stegs. The entire dale mourned its passing.

Sam was also a masterly shepherd and an expert breeder of Swaledale sheep, a most hardy animal which roams at will along the high fells and can live through all but the most brutal winters, even possessing the stamina to survive being buried for days under several feel of snow, so long as there is an air hole. The fells around Baldersdale are dangerous places, full of hidden ghylls – deep water holes – and moss bogs which can swallow a man whole. Sam knew every square inch of this territory, surefooted even on winter nights, and a recognized guide to those who had need to travel the moors. There was no one more adept at tracing and rescuing sheep trapped in snow drifts.

He could also play a variety of instruments (and passed on this ability to his children) and knew songs and melodies which had never been written down – just passed on from ear to ear via generations of Dalesmen. True folk music.

What a man he must have been. He has fittingly been given a measure of local immortality by Mrs Lavinia Mary Thwaites, who spent much time in the man's jovial company. Now retired and living in Cotherstone, she still glows at the memory of parties thrown by the Thwaites and the Fawcetts. She is a natural historian who has spent years researching and collecting information about Baldersdale and the surrounding area, delivering lectures to local societies and writing for Teesdale publications. She also possesses poetic talents. Sam Fawcett inspired her to these lines:

> The love of the hills has got into your blood,
>   The feel of the ling 'neath your feet.
> The call of the birds has made it seem good
>   As you carefully tended your sheep.
> With a bag well stocked with a loving fare,
>   Each morning you'd set on your round.
> With never a thought, be it near or far, 'ere,
>   the wandering lost sheep would be found.
> And out on the moors so lonely to those,
>   who seek the gay lights of the town.
> Where curlew and redshank and lapwing repose,
>   great peace and contentment you found.
> When the day's work was done and t'was Eventide,
>   You'd turn your face homeward and say,
> to the faithful old dog who walked by your side,
>   Well, Moses, we've had a most glorious day.

11

The 'Heirs' of Hannah

The impact made on the public by Hannah Hauxwell and *Too Long a Winter* has been well recorded and the lady herself must be on the permanent check list of every other news editor in the land. Constant references to Hannah are made in newspapers and her programmes often became a yardstick by which other documentaries were judged, particularly those made by the Yorkshire Television team which created it.

Yet *Too Long a Winter* was not entirely devoted to the story of Hannah Hauxwell. Indeed she scarcely figures in the programme until the second half. Most of the first half was devoted to a remarkable family called Bainbridge and their love-hate relationship with a farm called Birkdale, which some consider to be the biggest agricultural challenge in the Yorkshire Dales. The farmhouse crouches, as though in permanent search of shelter, in a hollow dominated by fells, which reach up to two thousand feet, close by where the counties of Yorkshire, Durham and Westmorland meet (the bureaucrats would challenge that assertion since they decided, for reasons best known to themselves, to mess around with the old boundaries – but just ask any local).

If you draw a direct line from Low Birk Hatt to Birkdale it would measure less than five miles, so Hannah and the Bainbridges are virtually neighbours. But it is seven miles from Birkdale to the nearest road – seven miles which are difficult enough in the middle of summer and frequently impossible in winter.

The first time Mary Bainbridge saw Birkdale she had emerged from a howling blizzard, having walked the seven miles with one child in her arms, another clinging on to her skirts and a third sitting on a horse-drawn sledge carrying the family furniture. Her husband had set his heart on this savage place when he first saw it as a teenager, working at a now defunct pyrites mine close to Birkdale, and saw it as a splendid area to

154

raise Swaledale sheep. Mary set about raising the children as Brian's flock multiplied satisfactorily to provide them with a living in their beautiful isolation. They lived happily there for seventeen years until one savage winter practically wiped out their livelihood. Three hundred and fifty sheep perished. Brian's laconic description of this catastrophe yielded the very title of 'Hannah's programme': 'It wasn't starvation that killed them, 'cause food was dropped by helicopter. It was just "too long a winter".'

'Too long a winter' – the phrase leapt from the screen when the rushes were viewed, although within days of transmission – and forever after at Yorkshire Television – the documentary was referred to simply as 'Hannah'. The Bainbridges, to all intents and purposes, sank without trace under the tidal wave of public fascination with Hannah. None of the gifts and ceaseless telephone calls was concerned with them, and out of sacksful of letters only half a dozen expressed any interest in their story, good though it was. One sequence showed Brian scrabbling with his bare hands deep down into a large drift of snow to locate, and haul to safety, a totally buried sheep. Powerful enough to have excited a fair amount of response from the public under normal circumstances but buried like the sheep under the Hannah Hauxwell avalanche.

All this did not escape the notice of the power-brokers of ITV. Neither did the reviews, which were ecstatic, even from the top, normally hard to please critics:

'Beautiful ... Hannah Hauxwell is Wordsworthian.' (Nancy Banks-Smith, *Guardian*)

'A marvellous Yorkshire documentary swept by fresh and haunting visual felicities ... Miss Hannah Hauxwell is a TV natural.' (Sean Day-Lewis, *Daily Telegraph*)

'Beautifully photographed...' (Peter Black, *Daily Mail*)

'A perfect example of a regional company striking gold in it's own back yard.' (Philip Purser, *Sunday Telegraph*)

'Nothing short of magical...' (*Daily Express*)

'Stark and stunning . . .' (*Daily Mirror*)

'Hannah Hauxwell, a saint . . .' (*Telegraph and Argus*, Bradford)

'Astonishing sequences . . .' (*Evening News*, London)

And Bob MacAlindin of the *Evening Express*, Aberdeen, who described it as 'a mini classic', made this remarkable declaration:

'Every now and then a television programme transcends the medium which carries it, and out of the technological tube in your living room filters something that strikes at life itself. In this case, it was a person . . . Hannah Hauxwell.'

This curious, tattered lady from out of nowhere became the criterion, the very touchstone for the *Too Long a Winter* production team, which was to stay together for more than a decade. She had transcended all the barriers of language and class. She was both universal and unique. There was no point in looking for more Hannahs. The task was, rather, to seek the essence of Hannah . . . to find people and situations which, however simple and unremarkable by accepted standards, nevertheless projected the eternal verities which humans in whatever condition could recognize instantly and then identify with.

That was the discipline the team obeyed as it went out to try and find the subjects to perpetuate this fragile, golden thread.

The heirs of Hannah Hauxwell came quickly to the ITV network screen.

The first successor was *Children of Eskdale*, about the Raw family living a glorious life in a superb farm on the North Yorkshire moors with their five bonny kids. The story line was simple – Dad wanted a tractor, the kids wanted a pony. The final sequence moved all those who watched it as John Raw secretly bought Prince, the pony he knew the children were besotted with, and quietly tethered it in the back pasture. Then he sent his eldest son, ten-year-old Alan Raw out on a spurious errand. Hidden cameras recorded the reaction of the children as they poured out of the back door to greet Prince, still only half believing it was really meant for them. It wasn't just their mother, Dot Raw, who cried at the sight of the pure joy of the children. To the somewhat less innocent joy of Yorkshire Television, this was also rapturously received by the public and critics alike. Nancy Banks-Smith, the finest essayist in Fleet Street, who could decorously lacerate a programme whilst ostensibly writing about the contents of her grandmother's handbag, ended her review with a declaration –

'A classic', she wrote.

Then came *Sunley's Daughter*, a love story set in the same stretch of high moorland along the banks of the Esk. This, and *The Dale that Died*, a stirring story from Upper Wensleydale, *A Chance in Life*, and others, were all received in a manner which stunned the production team. Although some were far from classics – indeed, one or two were fairly ordinary – the pattern was repeated every time the same team brought a programme to the screen. Enormous Press attention before and after transmission became standard (and led directly to large audiences), and the ghost of 'Saint' Hannah loomed over them all. Scarcely a newspaper piece about this new wave of documentaries, stretching over several years, failed to include a reference to the revered inhabitant of Low Birk Hatt Farm.

International attention, sales and acclaim followed swiftly, and so did the awards and honours. The most coveted in the world is the Prix Italia, and when a jury of twelve top television executives met to pick the British entry for 1974, six votes were cast for *Too Long a Winter* and five for *Children of Eskdale*. A single vote went to one of the batch of other nominees. So, 'Hannah' – the documentary, not the lady – went to Florence flying the Union Jack, and *Children of Eskdale* was granted an 'Honours Night', shown before a packed and extraordinarily appreciative audience on the giant screen at a Florentine cinema.

Too Long a Winter was also applauded after its showing in competition, the only film accorded that spontaneous honour – and was the very clear favourite to win the trophy. Unfortunately, it failed. There is a bitter theory about the reason. A worthy, if pedestrian, documentary from Japan was selected, a decision which even rendered the Japanese speechless. An Italian gentleman, exuding both importance and anger, approached the disconsolate Yorkshire Television contingent and said, 'Gentlemen, if you enter your marvellous film for the Trento Festival, I am sure it will win. Let me have a copy.' He was right. 'Hannah' went on to be honoured in New York in the Emmy Awards and ended with a clutch of *objets d'art* for the boardroom.

'Hannah' and her heirs played a leading role in establishing a documentary department which became internationally recognized for its standards of excellence.

Postscript

There is a season in the life of Hannah Hauxwell which has for years been urgently desired by those who care for her welfare. To retire … to leave Low Birk Hatt, to put behind her the punishing burden of running a farm totally unaided.

A small group of constant friends have watched, pleaded, waited and despaired as she turned their attempts at persuasion aside with typical courtesy and gentle phrases and then carried on, her physical condition visibly deteriorating, fighting a gradually losing battle with Low Birk Hatt, where every mid-winter is deep. It was frighteningly clear that each passing year sapped a little more of her remaining reserves of strength.

Her situation was precarious enough during her pre-television days when every penny had to be watched and she could only afford to keep one cow and its calf. The material benefits which come automatically with fame did not, regretfully, improve Hannah's daily regime on the farm. Indeed, they led directly to a significant increase in her workload as she invested in more cattle. Friends who waded thigh-deep through the drifts in January and February were horrified to find her painfully dragging loads of fodder on a sledge over the snow to feed this vastly expanded family (all fondly given a pet name). The sound of her rasping breath as she heaved herself and heavy bales over stone walls could be heard across two meadows.

All this led inevitably to a serious decline in the state of her living quarters. As Hannah herself is fond of saying, she has to be both the farmer and the farmer's wife. So the time available to attend to household duties such as cleaning, dusting and washing, etc., was dramatically depleted. Her cherished beasties came first . . . and second and third.

To be frank, Hannah's living conditions degenerated into a sorry mess. A dwelling once capable of housing seven people became so crowded with various objects, including parcels from all round the world (some of which appeared to be unopened) that movement was severely restricted. Hannah clings firmly on to things which are eminently disposable, such as bits of string, plastic bags and containers, brown paper, even empty beans tins. To throw anything away constituted an unforgivable waste, a state of mind doubtless conditioned by the memory of those early days when poverty, even the threat of malnutrition, was a very real factor. The situation became so bad that corridors had to be created through this confusion of items, so narrow that two people found it difficult to pass.

Cobwebs draped the ceiling and walls, dust lay thickly on most surfaces and wallpaper fell limply from the walls. Most rooms were colonized during the winter by mice – and rats. Rats are deadly. You can die from food polluted by rats, or even by placing your hand were one has urinated. Naturally, this created another major worry for those concerned about Hannah's safety.

Dimly perceptible through this spectacular untidiness, however, was the superb basic quality of a great deal of the furniture. One or more of Hannah's forebears must have possessed both good taste and the money to go with it, because they brought to Low Birk Hatt wardrobes and chests of drawers constructed in oak and mahogany by craftsmen of the old school. There were also case clocks, organs, four poster beds ornately carved, and much more; some a touch worm-eaten, but most well over a century old and clearly valuable as antiques.

All in all, Hannah was the sole owner of possessions which – if only she would sell up and escape – would yield enough capital to keep her in comfort. For, even if she sold her land and buildings at the lower end of a conservative valuation, there would be enough to buy a desirable dwelling in one of the villages near Baldersdale, with sufficient in hand to invest and supplement her pension.

So there was a measure of cautious rejoicing when, at the beginning of 1988, Hannah yielded in small measure to all those years of gentle persuasion by at least agreeing to look at properties on the books of Teesdale estate agents. Just to look, mind you . . . no commitment.

Then, in the spring of that year she was attracted by a cottage on sale in Mickleton. It answered all the complex requirements outlined by Hannah when she described the type of property which may – just may, mind – incline her towards leaving Low Birk Hatt. The cottage in question had two and a half acres of pastureland which meant she could take Rosa, the senior cow, along with her. She would even have room for a few hens and a goat. The place was detached and had some very useful outbuildings, including a stone-built stable just right for Rosa's winter quarters. Such matters were clearly as important as the two bedrooms, lounge, dining room, kitchen and utility room and the luxury of water on tap.

The cottage was due to be publicly auctioned at the Kings Head Hotel, Barnard Castle, and Hannah agonized for a week over the top price she would bid. Not that she would attend the auction in person – that would be no place for a maiden lady of delicate disposition. A group of eager friends, delighted at the momentous decision, agreed to represent her. One of them, a man experienced in the local property market and who had wide knowledge of the pitfalls, was selected to do the bidding. It became clear that Hannah had set her heart on this property as over the last four days before the auction, she raised her top offer every day. As the party departed for the Kings Head she whispered into the ear of a confidante that another five hundred pounds could be added, if it became absolutely necessary.

But for an unfortunate quirk of fate, the property would now be Hannah's new home. Her final bid was sufficient to beat all local opposition, but a couple said to be moving back to Teesdale after a spell in the London area were obviously prepared to go much higher than the expected price. It was assumed they considered the cottage, knocked down at £36,000, to be rather cheap when compared with south-eastern prices. They and Hannah were the last two bidders.

Hannah accepted the bad news philosophically. The friends seemed to register more distress, because they realized that through sheer bad luck, a very rare opportunity had been missed.

As the summer of 1988 slipped damply and miserably away, the gloom of the Hannah Hauxwell Supporters' Club deepened perceptibly. There were no further signals from Low Birk Hatt that the lady was contemplating any other property. There was, however, one very ominous signal from another quarter – that the winter of 1988/9 could be a really bad one.

'We're due one . . . all the signs are there,' said local opinion. The potential accuracy of this sombre forecast was reinforced in autumn when the temperature dipped below zero and snow-ploughs churned through to keep the roads of Baldersdale open.

If there was to be a repeat of the 1978/9 agony, when the power failed, her clothes became sheet ice on her back and the sole source of warm nourishment was Rosa's milk, there would be serious doubts about Hannah's ability to survive.

For heaven's sake, apart from everything else, she suffers from angina . . .

Then it happened – and no one is quite sure how or when she made her decision. Frankly, her friends had run out of variations on the old theme of the desperate urgency to get out of Low Birk Hatt and were directing their energies towards plans to cope with the emergencies to come. But, quite unexpectedly, she announced her intention to bid for a cottage in Cotherstone, recently placed on the market. There was to be no auction this time, just the usual private negotiation through an estate agent.

Belle Vue Cottage is ideally suited to Hannah's needs, situated in the middle of an attractive Dales village. There is a combined post office and shop which sells the famous Cotherstone cheese, another shop with petrol pumps, two pubs (not that Hannah will have much need of them) and a friendly population – and readily available medical facilities.

Negotiations for the property went like a dream. The lively octoganerian who owned Belle Vue Cottage (and was moving further north to be near her relatives) turned out to be one of the vast army of Hannah 'fans'. She was so delighted that her meticulously maintained and cherished home was favoured by Hannah that she attempted to drop the price (and this in an area where property had recently been known to attract bids over and above the asking price). It is safe to assume that anyone else interested was not encouraged. When the sale was agreed, the news spread like a moorland grass fire throughout Cotherstone.

Hannah was coming to live there! Delight was widespread, particularly among some ladies who once lived themselves in Baldersdale and knew Hannah from the old days. However, it was nothing compared to the monumental relief felt by the people who had worked towards this for more years than they cared to recall.

A support team moved into action immediately. It was led by Kathy Rooney (who was helping to produce the latest television documentary) and Richard Megson (who runs the youth hostel in Baldersdale and has long been the selfless helper on the spot). Mightily did they labour. Day by day they guided Hannah through the valuation and sale of her property, organizing estate agents, solicitors, bank managers, removal companies and getting to personal grips with the huge task of clearing out the amazing contents of Low Birk Hatt (a glance at the photograph in this book of Hannah sitting among her belongings will convey the scene better than the proverbial thousand words).

It went on for weeks, complicated as it was by Hannah's innate reluctance, born of earlier deprivation, to throw anything away on the grounds that 'one never knows when it might come in useful'. Many items of dubious value were retained for later dispatch to Cotherstone, but eventually the night sky of Baldersdale was illuminated by the flames of a large bonfire built from several decades of rubbish.

As one would expect, a crisis developed over the beloved beasts. There was no room for Rosa at Belle Vue Cottage, and the thought of the senior cow and all her progeny going to goodness knows what fate at the auction mart was totally unacceptable. A loyal friend and neighbour, Bill Purves of Clove Lodge, agreed to take them on and assured Hannah that he would care for them as she would wish.

The final parting was not a happy time. Those who witnessed it were visibly affected themselves as Hannah bade farewell one misty afternoon. She watched them disappear through the iron gate and down the new road, her face white and wet with distress.

Hannah took most of her best furniture to Cotherstone, and there was precious little to put into the farm sale since Low Birk

Hatt boasted none of the modern equipment other farms possess. Some stone troughs, a few scythes and rakes, a quantity of horse-drawn equipment, but not much else. Nevertheless, more than two hundred people (plus film crews, reporters and photographers) trudged through the glutinous mud to be there, and Clifford Pratt, an archetypal Dales auctioneer from Hawes in Upper Wensleydale, conducted the sale with gravelly skill. His understated, classic Northern humour helped to spur occasional spirited bidding. Some of the four poster beds, tables and other antique pieces which would not fit into Belle Vue Cottage yielded useful sums and the overall sale result exceeded expectations.

The sealed bids for the farmhouse and land were equally satisfactory. The one which caused deepest pleasure in Hannah was from a conservation organization which had spotted that one particular parcel of her land was so unspoiled and unpolluted by artificial fertilizers that it was virtually unique for miles around, a haven for rare grasses and wild flowers.

This land will be kept in exactly the way Hannah kept it, the way her ancestors kept it for centuries, and it will be named after her.

Hannah is too private a person to disclose publicly the sum she accepted for her property but after paying in full for her new home and all expenses, it seems certain that her future is secure – financially, at least. A revolutionary concept when compared to the years she spent living well below the lowest of subsistence levels.

Now ... it all sounds like a happy ending fashioned by a romantic novelist. But a very real trauma remains. All those who stayed by her side during this latest season in the remarkable life of Hannah Bayles Tallentire Hauxwell know it.

They saw her sitting in the one remaining chair in a house hollow with emptiness after the farm sale, so deep in an unspoken grief that everyone and everything else could have been a thousand miles away.

They saw her in the cab of the removal van as it was dragged by tractor out of the snow and ice of Baldersdale, clutching her dog, Timmy, and staring with unseeing eyes at the spectacular

Hannah finds a quiet corner during the auction of her belongings (Press Association)

sunset gilding the shimmering waters of the Mississippi, her name for the sinuous reservoir over which Low Birk Hatt perches.

There is central heating, a flush toilet, hot running water and – Lord help us! – an ex-directory telephone awaiting her in Cotherstone.

But as the winter of 1988/9 closed in, there was no doubt where the heart of Hannah is lodged, now and possibly forever:

Low Birk Hatt, Baldersdale.

> *'Wherever I go . . . and whatever I am . . .*
> *this is me . . .'*

Part Two
Daughter of the Dales

Preface
The Leaving of Hannah

I don't know how I'll leave here . . . or how I'll feel after I have left. It will be a big upheaval, emotionally . . . physically . . . mentally . . .

It's just as though my world is falling to pieces. Everything I have known and been sure of . . . security, everything . . .

When Hannah Hauxwell made her reluctant exit from Baldersdale it was as if the elements conspired to invest it with special meaning. The entire valley shimmered with a glacial beauty as a four-wheel-drive-tractor, hazard light flashing, began to drag a hapless furniture van laden with her belongings out of its wild embrace.

Very few people saw snow that mild and benevolent winter but Baldersdale was not about to let its most cherished daughter go without a final salute.

It was a classic set piece encompassing all the glory – and the pain – of the place. The snow had fallen in unreasonable amounts and every corner was illuminated by that particular light which blesses the remoter regions where the air is unpolluted, casting an iridescent mantle which made the waters of Hunder Beck and the reservoir that feeds it dance like quicksilver. The same light silhouetted the farmhouse and the tall trees around it: Low Birk Hatt, home to the Hauxwells since it was built and the place where Hannah's spirit will always reside.

To me there's nowhere like it and never will be. This is my life – my world. And in years to come, if you see a funny old person – a ghost – walking up and down, it will be me.

And then came the concluding flourish.

As the convoy toiled upwards along the winding track, scattering sheep with icicled fleeces in its wake, a molten sunset began to spill slowly across the skyline.

Hannah left it all without a backward glance as though, in classic Homeric fashion, she knew she had to shut out the siren call. She sat in the cab of the van as if turned to stone, eyes glazed with tears.

She says she will never go back.

Wherever I am, whatever I am, a big part of me will be left here. Nowhere else . . .

That poignant moment in Hannah's life, that final severance of the chains which had bound her to Baldersdale far too long for her physical well-being, was essentially a private matter. Yet it was eventually shared by almost six and a half million people.

Tucked discreetly away behind a deep-frozen hillock, observing and recording the mournful event, was a camera crew, hardly believing their professional good fortune as nature turned on that slow-motion firework display.

For one man – the writer of this piece – there was a distinct sense of *déjà vu*. He had been there almost exactly seventeen years before, standing alongside a camera not very far from the same position, directing the very first film sequence ever shown of Hannah Bayles Tallentire Hauxwell.

Just like that afternoon, Baldersdale was deep in snow – indeed, a blizzard was blowing at the time.

And the scene was backlit by a stunning sunset.

And Hannah was towing a milk-white cow.

The first sequence . . . and now, almost two decades later, the last sequence. Two nearly identical situations. But so much had happened in between. Three major, internationally transmitted television documentaries, two best-selling books.

And the creation of a legend.

No one could have forecast the explosion of public interest created when Hannah emerged from that blizzard – and total obscurity – in the first Yorkshire Television programme, *Too*

Hannah with Barry Cockcroft during the making of Too Long a Winter *in 1972*

Long a Winter. That was remarkable enough but the way in which she moved with sublime serenity into a permanent position in the affections of a public which stretches far beyond the frontiers of this country was truly astonishing.

The most unlikely celebrity of them all transmits an aura which is almost royal in its nature. Everything she does or says automatically attracts the attention of an enormous audience. Every time she makes a public appearance the crowds turn out and queue for hours for a chance to get close to her. And some of her admirers are almost too awestruck to speak when they are finally face to face with the lady.

If you try to analyse this phenomenon coldly and clinically, it all seems a total aberration. For instance, the third and final documentary, *A Winter Too Many*, had a storyline which would have been laughed to scorn under normal circumstances. A full hour of network time devoted to some elderly lady in a half-abandoned dale trying to decide whether or not to leave her farm and go into a retirement cottage?

Totally ridiculous!

But that programme was hailed as the most popular of the year. Over 6 million people watched – more than double the average for a late-night documentary – and, judging from the response it drew, a fair proportion could scarcely see for tears. The mail certainly flooded in, all exceedingly appreciative and most demanding a repeat. Even before that success, Hannah was firmly fixed in the celebrity rota of the Press, which monitors her progress constantly and sends its best writers to pen a stream of in-depth interviews (and even the most hardboiled and cynical of them melt in the warmth of her simple honesty).

Hannah's journey from the deprivation of the years alone and unknown, working a merciless hill farm, living on the pitiful sum of £280 a year (and paying for animal-feed out of that), with no basic amenities such as electricity or water on tap, via an unprecedented tidal wave of public adulation, to that heart-rending farewell to the place she holds so dear, has been a self-perpetuating saga unique in the annals of modern folklore.

And now the story of Hannah Hauxwell moves into another phase: the next chapter of a life which has fascinated thousands of people from all sectors of the social spectrum, who see in this lady a quality so fundamental and inspirational that it transcends all barriers and casts a spell which cannot conclusively be explained.

1

Hannah's New Life: Coping with Civilization – and The Great One

It was clear that Hannah would not consider moving far from her native heath and, after lengthy deliberations, settled on a cottage in Cotherstone which stands five miles away from Low Birk Hatt at one of the entrances to Baldersdale. It's a well-founded Dales village, mentioned in the Domesday Book, with a fascinating and somewhat turbulent, if bizarre, history. Cotherstone Castle, which loomed over the confluence of the rivers Tees and Balder, is now just a heap of rubble. But it certainly saw some action. Last occupied in 1315, it was the ancestral home of the Fitzhughs but passed by marriage out of the family when the last of the male line died in a hunting accident while pursuing his quarry clean over a cliff, if local legend is correct. Then the Scots raided down from the borders and put it to the torch. A lot of the stone went to build houses for the local peasants, who apparently had a tough time. They were once so poverty-stricken they were known through the valley of the Tees as people who 'christened calves, hoppled lops and knee-banded spiders'. That meant they could afford so few cattle that each one had a name (a tradition perpetuated by Hannah!), and lops (lice) and spiders had their legs tied together to prevent them running away.

The area suffered badly during the time of the plague, which gave rise to the legend of the Butterstone. It stands in splendid isolation near the moorland road to Bowes and it was there that merchants and farmers would leave butter, eggs and other foodstuffs to be picked up by the afflicted. They were obliged to leave their money in a bowl of vinegar to – it was hoped – ward off contamination.

Life proceeds at a gentle, traditional pace today for the 500 or so residents of Cotherstone. Kelvin Walker runs his general store and petrol pumps (and taxi service), the Post Office also sells the superb Cotherstone cheese, and there are two excellent public houses.

Belle Vue Cottage is very conveniently situated for all these amenities, and a distinct *frisson* of excitement ran through the community when it became known that Hannah Hauxwell was the new owner.

Now, it's a funny thing, but in the days when there was a weekly bus service out of Baldersdale it went past Belle Vue cottage on the way to Barnard Castle and I used to look at it and say to myself, 'Well, that's an ugly place, I wouldn't like to live there!'

I don't wish to be disrespectful, and everybody has a right to their own taste, but it was the colour of it that really put me off. It was painted in a kind of orange. Someone obviously agreed with me eventually and it was changed to its present cream colour, which is a vast improvement.

Oddly enough, I had been interested in it three or four years ago when it was on the market prior to being bought by the lady who sold it to me. I was being taken somewhere by car and a stop had been made at Kelvin's petrol pumps opposite. There was a 'For Sale' sign outside, and at the time I was beginning to contemplate leaving Baldersdale – half of me wanted a more suitable place and the other half was telling me to stop at Low Birk Hatt. So I had a look at it from the outside and I changed my original opinion. It seemed to have a good deal going for it.

But the one thing that you cannot change, unlike the colour, is the fact that it faces north. Most of the living accommodation at Low Birk Hatt faces north and I always thought that when I moved I would definitely have a south-facing house. I didn't fancy north again at all. But there is a saying, is there not: 'Man proposes, and God disposes!'

What it does have – and this is a very important thing for me, having lived for so many years in an isolated place – is a certain amount of privacy. When one has been used to the nearest neighbours being several fields away, it wouldn't do to have someone else's door or window overlooking every part of the house. The whole of one side of Belle Vue Cottage is quite private, and I count that a real blessing.

The other factor that appealed to me was the size of the

rooms. They are very nicely proportioned for a cottage. The lounge has a large bay window with a beautiful view of the village and I can sit there and watch the world go by, if I feel like it.

And then I have always fancied a little hall and stairs because at the farm the stairs came straight down to the front door. Now I have stairs which actually turn the corner into a splendid hall. You get less draughts that way.

There are two good-sized bedrooms and a box-room but the real luxury is the bathroom. I never had such a thing before, and I am like a child when it comes to running water. Mind, I can always claim to have had running water at Low Birk Hatt but it did happen to be a stream some way down the meadow. When you've been used to that for sixty-two years, hot water and a flushing toilet do come as something of a culture shock.

Then there is the telephone. Until I arrived here I tended to regard the telephone with some trepidation. It took a good deal of time for me and it to get together. I used to wonder what on earth people found to talk about for so long, and on the occasion when I was called to a neighbour's telephone in Baldersdale, I was so uneasy that someone had to hold it to my ear. But that has all changed now. I find it a very useful thing, and I am as bad as the next person at chatting merrily away with little thought of time or the expense of it. If there is one drawback to life at Belle Vue Cottage, it is the lack of land around the place. There is a small strip of garden at the front but nothing at the back or side, not even a yard. I have to rely on the kindness of a good neighbour to hang out my washing. But I came to terms with all that because the house has so much going for it in other ways.

Small it may be, but that postage stamp of a garden at the front of the house does boast a distinction which falls to but a few: two rose bushes of a rather particular, not to say exclusive, variety.

I must admit that my first few days in my new home were quite strange and a little frightening. I kept hearing these small explosions and I wondered what could possibly be the

A view of old Cotherston (sic) (Courtesy of Darlington Library)

cause. Then I cottoned on that it was the gas central-heating boiler coming on. It's such a wonderful thing and gives out such heat that I spend quite a lot of my time sitting alongside it in the kitchen. It seems to have a mind of its own, and I call it The Great One.

Mrs Pearson, the nice old lady who sold Belle Vue Cottage to me, set the controls a few days before she left and said the milkman understood how it worked and he would help me if I had need of it. Now I am not at one with technology such as electricity and things like that. Unless it is an easy switch-on or switch-off I tend to be lost. I am more geared to old things, and

177

Hannah's cottage – a summer view

The Great One does play some funny tricks sometimes. It once went cold, although the little red lights were still on. I didn't bother the milkman, but a lady kindly came and put in a little battery – and then the neighbours adjusted it and got it going. I still haven't a clue how it works.

I also have an automatic washing machine but it has to be by the sink for the water to be pumped out and it has no wheels. So I still wash by hand with my blue-bag and my plunger. There's a little spin-dryer too, but I haven't got around to using that either.

Now Mrs Pearson was most kind to me over the sale of the house – indeed, but for her kindness I would probably never have got it. Several people were after it, but when she knew I wanted it she sent a message saying she preferred me to have it. I think maybe she had seen the television programmes and was favourably disposed.

I finally moved in just before Christmas 1988 and, like Edith Piaf, I have no regrets. Everyone in the village is most friendly.

One problem is the constant flow of visitors who arrive unannounced on my doorstep. They are all very welcome, of course, although they park their cars in inconvenient places, but they do not help in the problems I have in finding the time to sort out my new home. Most of my stuff is still in packing-cases and, because I am not a very quick person, it is likely I will remain in a disorganized state for some time to come. Of course, I have this terrible failing: I am a hoarder. I cannot bear to throw things away, partly because of my upbringing and partly out of sentiment.

I suppose I have enough to fill two cottages, so space is at a premium before I have even unpacked half of what I brought. One very generous gentleman in London, who imports pianos from Poland and who heard me playing the organ in the programmes, has offered me a brand-new piano as a gift. I would like to have it very much because music is one of the great pleasures in life to me but I just have nowhere to put it at the moment.

There are so many demands on my time. Quite apart from my visitors and my new friends, some of whom whisk me away to stay for the weekend, there are what you could call my 'professional engagements'. By that I mean book-signing sessions – I've been all over the place, from Darlington and Beverley in the North, to as far as Nottingham in the South, and met some wonderful people – and literary luncheons, plus what I suppose you could call 'personal appearances' at all kinds of functions.

So it is very difficult to achieve what one might call a set pattern in life. Back at Low Birk Hatt there was no such problem because the demands of the seasons, and particularly the daily needs of my animals – my family, as you could call them – filled every waking moment.

On the days when I am left to my own devices I am a bit of a disgrace really. I get up at a rather late hour. Indeed I have my breakfast at dinner-time, somewhere around 11.30 a.m. – that's the time for the main meal of the day in farming circles since it is normal for those who live from the land to rise at first light. Now, I was never a good getter-up but I do have the excuse that I often retire very late, particularly if I have a visitor in the afternoon and need to get a bit of washing or something done at night when it is possible to get on with it without interruptions. All in all, I suppose I have changed to something of a nightbird. There is a good social life in the village, and I wish I had a chance to become more involved. I have been to the Over-Sixties Club where they have some very good concerts and I go to services at Cotherstone Methodist Chapel whenever I can.

There is no routine. I suppose routines and me don't go together.

2

Health, Wealth... and the Perils of Civilization

Hannah Hauxwell's somewhat late introduction to the benefits of modern civilization, such as water that arrived at the turn of a tap, central heating, shops just a few yards away, even a telephone (the number is ex-directory or it would never stop), clearly created a revolution in her life. Her financial situation also improved dramatically, with a tidy amount left from the sale of Low Birk Hatt to invest, and substantial sums from the royalties of her best-selling book. But what no one could foresee were the complex problems of readjustment. For instance, the emotional strain of leaving Baldersdale almost certainly reduced her resistance to the germs and viruses that also come with the overall package of civilization. Less than a year after her arrival in Cotherstone, a crisis occurred.

It started on a Friday night in November when I felt a bit odd, so I took a Paracetamol and went to bed with a hot-water bottle. Next day I didn't feel so bad and I made an appearance for a charity – I really had to do it – then went to visit a relative the following day. But by the Tuesday night my throat had all dried up and, though I tried to motor on, I had to take to my bed on the Wednesday. I thought it would only take a couple of days to clear up, but it was to take quite a lot longer.

I'm afraid that when I dropped out of sight it created a great deal of concern in the village. A friend who had a key let herself in and called upstairs, but I didn't want anyone to come into the bedroom because they might catch whatever it was I had. And I didn't want to bother with a doctor – in Baldersdale you were used to dealing with minor complaints on your own. But as time dragged on and I obviously got worse, I suppose my friends decided to take action. A doctor was called out and he diagnosed some kind of virus and prescribed a course of antibiotics.

That should have been the end of it but it most certainly was not. Altogether it lasted a month and but for the neighbours rallying around and taking care of me I would have ended up in hospital.

For day after day I couldn't even keep water down. Everything tasted horrible. But Elsie Birdsall and Lavinia Thwaites kept coming in with all kinds of things to try and get me going – home-made soups, arrowroot, custards – and finally I began to mend a little.

I know one or two people had begun to despair of me ever getting better at one point but, basically, I have been blessed with a strong constitution. There are one or two worries, such as the blood pressure and a touch of angina. And I suppose it might have been serious had I been at Low Birk Hatt on my own with no help when that virus struck me down. But then, the air is purer and germs less prevalent there.

I did get the usual childhood ailments, though, such as mumps, measles and chicken-pox. So Baldersdale wasn't that free of infection. Mind, I welcomed them with open arms because it meant I could stay off school. But one summer when I was around ten or eleven I developed a nasty sore throat which the doctor thought was tonsillitis. Then I started to be sick and my skin started to peel and drop off. You see, it turned out to be scarlet fever, which is a notifiable disease. But by the time everyone, including the doctor, realized what it was it was just too late. Mother had told Mrs Archer at Baldersdale school that it was tonsillitis and I'm not sure that she ever did find out the reality of it. As far as I know, no one else in the Dale caught it – except my Uncle Tommy, my father's brother who had come to run the farm for us when my father died at such a tragically early age. I think we must have both picked it up during a visit to some relatives in Pierce-bridge.

It was Mother who nursed us through it and it was an experience I wouldn't like to repeat. It took about six weeks for the fever to go and then we got sulphur candles to fumigate the house from top to bottom. I suppose if the doctor had got his diagnosis right, then I would have had to go to hospital but it was to be another ten years before I was sent to such a place.

A rare picture of Hannah, recently unearthed, taken shortly after her mother's death in 1958

I had been poorly for a while and couldn't eat and the doctor thought it may be appendicitis so he sent me to Darlington Hospital. I was scared at the prospect of an operation but, thankfully, it didn't prove necessary. I didn't like hospital at all that time because such strange things happened in the night with nurses coming and going and moving people and giving injections. In fact, in the middle of one night they came and moved my bed to another part of the hospital without saying a word to me.

The next time I needed serious medical attention was quite a

184

different experience. I had just had my forty-first birthday and had been going through a very unhappy time, not eating properly because I was economizing so much, and becoming properly run down. Of course, by then I was completely on my own and the doctor told me that I must go into hospital – this time at Northallerton.

They were ever so grand there. I went in feeling very poorly and not much good for anything and came out a new woman. Mind, it took about eight weeks to achieve that desirable state, and all they did was to give me some tablets, good food, rest and lots of kindness. I should have been discharged earlier but I had developed a cold and they insisted I stay until it had completely cleared up.

I met some wonderful people in that place. There was one lady with a very posh voice, a doctor's widow, who had been in Jarrow at the time of that terrible hunger march. She was a big woman and had suffered a stroke. I noticed that she looked a bit unhappy so I went across to her, worried that she might be a bit of a madam and wouldn't like to associate with the likes of me. But we became the firmest of friends and kept in touch by letter afterwards until she sadly died. There were several others who used to come and see me in Baldersdale, particularly after the first television programme went out in January 1973, including some of the nurses. They were so marvellous those nurses, some of them so young and all so dedicated. I think nurses are born, not made. Speaking of television, I had my first taste of the magic box in that hospital. They allowed us to watch it in the dayroom until 10.00 p.m. But, to be honest, I wasn't that keen. I have to admit I was sorry to leave Northallerton Hospital. It was lonely when I came back to Low Birk Hatt.

Now, as far as my health is concerned these days it could be a little bit better but a bonny sight worse. I take pills every day for my blood pressure, and I have some others, little things, ready for when I get what I call chuntering pains in my chest. And there's a bit of rheumatism in my right shoulder and arm which is something of a nuisance. When I was convalescing after that last virus, my Good Samaritans in Cotherstone arranged for me to have the Meals on Wheels service for several weeks. They were excellent and built up my strength nicely.

Even before that I had put on some weight which didn't all drain away during my illness. I don't know what I weigh now, but I can tell from the mirror and the clothes that I wear that there is, sadly, more of me than there was.

It could be about twelve years ago since I last weighed myself. There weren't many weighing machines in Baldersdale, but then a friend had to get one because of health problems and I turned out to be something around ten stones. Goodness knows what it is now.

I have friends who worry that I don't eat well and regularly enough but I suppose it is all a continuation of the habits formed when I was a one-woman farmer. I always like butter and toast for my breakfast – never bacon because that is a dinner dish. Sometimes dinner comes and sometimes it does not. It all depends on the time I can find to prepare it. During the hot summers I've had a lot of lettuce and tomato with maybe a bit of fruit. Last summer I really lived it up because I treated myself to some peaches.

And now I find myself eating tomatoes in the winter, which must be considered something of a luxury.

But it seems that I cannot rid myself of this fear of running short of money. It is in the system and has been for as long as I can recall. I know that I have a comfortable income now, but I still have difficulty in believing it. The brake is still on financially. I tend to live on my pension and, even when I see something I need, I will try and think of a reason to manage without.

For instance, in Kelvin Walker's shop across the road there are some brushes that I need. I'll ask him all about them and look at them but I keep putting off buying them. I know it seems like madness, but it's something I just cannot help.

The artist Trevor Stubley at work on a portrait of Hannah which was exhibited at the National Portrait Gallery

If you ask me how I would indulge myself if forced to, I suppose I would put some comfortable footwear near the top of the list. Then perhaps some joints of meat, or a fowl. I cannot do it yet but I am trying to come round to it. One is constantly reminded that life is short, so I suppose I should. But then I don't do too badly, and people mustn't worry so much about me.

3

Hannah's Secrets... and the Return of Rosa, the Senior Cow

Like all maiden ladies, Hannah Hauxwell has her secrets. And she can spring a surprise. Not long after acquiring Belle Vue Cottage she began to search for a piece of land in the Cotherstone area, preferably a fenced-in meadow. It soon became a matter of urgency. Puzzled friends were informed, as they set about helping her to find something, that it was necessary to afford Hannah some privacy – somewhere the daily stream of visitors wouldn't know about, somewhere she could escape to and sit and dream in solitude. But it transpired eventually that wasn't the only reason. Those who saw her last television programme, *A Winter Too Many*, will remember the extremely poignant sequence – and the tears – when she said farewell to her 'family', the beloved beasts, as they wended their way down the road from Low Birk Hatt to new ownership, led by the senior cow – 'Rosa, my lovely Rosa' – who had given Hannah the only available warm drink, her milk, and acted as a radiator when the power failed at Low Birk Hatt during the last savage winter. Well, it turned out that Rosa wasn't sold at all. She still belongs to Hannah, and is merely boarding out. Eventually, some land was found, and the lady who finds it psychologically impossible for the moment to afford a piece of meat parted with a substantial sum without demur.

I hope people will understand when I say I don't want to reveal exactly where it is. The need to have my own quiet corner became a priority during my first Easter in Cotherstone, when I was a bit depressed. I was suffering from a cold, the first for years – in fact I cannot recall the last time I had a cold – and because the weather was nice the village was extremely busy with tourists and lots of traffic and people knocking on my door. I thought to myself that I had landed up in a place without an inch of ground to call my own.

Now please understand that I really do like my visitors.

They are, with few exceptions, very kind and generous and come from far and near, even from overseas. Some have become true friends, and I have spent several weekends away because of their thoughtfulness. One couple who own an apartment in the south of Spain are even trying to persuade me to go there. But to travel to foreign parts is something I have never done and can scarcely contemplate. But the time might come!

They keep on calling me a celebrity, but I cannot really accept that. I am just an ordinary Daleswoman and if I began to think or act otherwise I know a few people around here who would soon bring me to my senses. But I have to concede that an amazing number of people are interested in me because of the television programmes and the books. Everyone needs a bit of time to themselves so something had to be done.

I was very lucky to find this piece of land. It's only about a quarter of an acre, but it's quite idyllic, and within reasonable reach of home. And I might be able to bring down Rosa for a bit during the summertime so we can renew our friendship. But I'm not sure whether it can be a permanent home for her because the fencing might not be good enough if she becomes lonely and tries to get out. Most animals like company, you know.

Quite apart from Rosa, it is necessary for me to have somewhere to go and think without interruption. Even if the weather is bad I'll still be able to slip away there because it has a shelter which was included in the sale.

I do miss Rosa, and I am not able to go and see her because she is being looked after by my friend, Bill Purves at Clove Lodge, the next farm to Low Birk Hatt. I am afraid I cannot bear just yet to go back to Baldersdale. Nor have I been able to watch *A Winter Too Many*.

I have thought about going up to Clove Lodge in the dark to say hello to Rosa, when I wouldn't be able to see my old place. You have to understand that no one but my family had ever lived at Low Birk Hatt before I sold it. My great-grandfather, William Bayles, was the first to occupy it and he was born in 1826. To go back and see it now might just upset the balance of

things at a crucial time, when I am trying to make a very difficult adjustment to my life.

I still have a foothold in Baldersdale, which is not widely known. Further down the valley from Low Birk Hatt is a place I own called Walker Hall, which has 17 acres of land. I was just not prepared to let that go when I sold Low Birk Hatt because it was my parents' dream house. They were going to retire there.

You see, they never really had a place of their own. They always had to share with other people, our elderly relatives. Walker Hall was bought long ago by Daddy's mother, Grandma Hauxwell, when she and Grandad were living at Hury in a place called Yew Tree. They never actually moved in and they promised it to Daddy.

Walker Hall may well be one of the oldest houses in Baldersdale. I believe it had a thatched roof and it was such a bonny place, but it has sadly been derelict for years. The last family to live there was called Wright, but that was well before my time.

It faces south, and had a little garden with trees all around. The thatched roof went long ago, but when I was a child the loft was still covered and Mother and Father kept a bed there and a few other necessary things. The three of us used to go down in summer to stay and do the haymaking. It's a lovely memory. Mother would cook on an open fire, the birds sang in the trees, and there was a bush in the corner which had white blossom, and roses grew wild everywhere. We all slept in the same bed, and it was so cosy.

I liked the design of the place very much. It had a nice square kitchen with one long window and a little narrow one, both with stone lintels. The kitchen opened into a very pleasant sitting-room, which had a door leading to a little dairy on the right and then to the stairs which had a half-landing with a tiny window looking out at the back. I think the

A discreet view of Hannah's hiding place – the small field where she hopes Rosa the cow may come to visit

Haytime in Baldersdale – the Hind family of Clove Lodge, once Hannah's neighbours. Probably taken between the wars.

stairs were constructed of stone but it's hard to tell because it's been deep in rubble ever since I can recall. There were two good bedrooms, both with fireplaces, and I believe another small one over the dairy. The door of the back kitchen went down two steps and then there was a chimney corner with shaped stonework, which I think would have had a wooden seat long ago.

Although there was – still is – a tree growing through the middle of the house, the stone walls had been well built and still stand to this day. Daddy was going to rebuild it with his own hands and had already done a bit to it when I was young. He put in a little stone trough to catch the water from a stream at the back, and bought a fireplace with an iron range oven and grate, especially for Walker Hall. He and Mother must have thought a great deal of the place to go to that expense at a time when money was so short.

Daddy had so many plans for Walker Hall but then he had so little time to do much. He died of pneumonia about twelve years after he bought Low Birk Hatt.

He was only thirty-seven.

194

4

Hard Life and the
Hauxwells:
the Untold Story of Hannah's
Mother and Father

'The Hard Life' – that was the television series title of *Too Long a Winter*. People were totally amazed that, in Britain in the second half of the twentieth century, someone could be living in such materially deprived conditions, alone, with no water on tap and no electricity, on an income of barely £5 a week – and that she could rise above it with such dignity, inner tranquillity and gentle philosophy.

And yet, the burden of life that her mother and father, separately and together, had to bear far exceeds that which Hannah endured, and may explain in some measure the genesis of Hannah's fortitude and sublime character, which have inspired so many.

Hannah may have gone without most of the comforts that people take for granted, but at least she had emotional warmth and stability, wrapped as she was in the cocoon of a caring family – her mother, grandparents, and for a little time her tragic father, all around her.

Not so her mother and father. Their lives were far more than just hard. And there were strange parallels in the patterns of their childhood. Hannah has never told their story before . . .

Father was a Baldersdale man, born and bred, brought up at Hury, lower down the Dale. Grandfather James Hauxwell met Grandmother Elizabeth, who was a Bayles, when he came to work on the building of the reservoir, just below Low Birk Hatt. He had been in the Army, had served in India, and knew a bit about the world. Although I loved him dearly, he was a bit of a rascal and liked the drink far too much. They took Yew Tree Farm at Hury, next to Walker Hall, and then moved to Nelson House. They had two sons, my father and Uncle Tommy, and I think another child who didn't survive.

Now, there was a bachelor brother of Grandmother's, my Great-Uncle Isaac, who had a farm called Dummah Hill at

North Stainmore. I imagine the family considered that my father would be better off living with him because of the atmosphere created by my grandfather's drinking. Daddy must have been quite young when he left, because he went to school at North Stainmore.

Oddly enough, a similar thing happened to my mother. Her mother, my Grandmother Anne, was a Sayers, and they were the Manor House family in Bowes and rather better off than most. They may even have had servants, and I remember seeing photographs of her in a beautiful gown. Sadly, I only ever saw my grandmother a couple of times so I never came to know her. She married into the Tallentire family, who owned the pub called New Spittal in the same area but relinquished the licence because of their Methodist beliefs. But the Tallentires were farmers and used to the physical hardships that go hand-in-hand with life on the land. Not that they didn't have an appreciation of the arts because they were a very musical family. And it was generally accepted that Grandad William Tallentire was capable of making his way in any society, so it really wasn't a clear case of Grandma marrying beneath her. The pub they used to have was patronized by shooting parties in the grouse season and one big businessman was so impressed by Grandad that he offered to take him back with him to train him for a position in his firm. But nothing came of it in the end.

Becoming a farmer's wife must have been very difficult for Grandma. She was rather young when she married and had been brought up as a lady, so it was another world for her. I can really sympathize with the situation in which she found herself. Then the children started coming along – rather quickly, I fear, and seven in number, which didn't help matters one bit. Her health began to suffer, which was understandable, and I think at one time she deteriorated so badly that the doctors rather washed their hands of her. But Grandad Tallentire persevered and nursed her through. So when Grandad's uncle, Richard Tallentire, asked if they could bring Mother up, they agreed to let her go. I believe she was very young – just a little thing – but it must have seemed the

North Stainmore School. Hannah's father in Eton collar, back row, behind the long-haired girl in white dress.

best thing to do in the circumstances. You see, Richard and his wife, Elizabeth, known as Aunt Bessie, had lost the only child they ever had. He was a little boy called Thomas Isaac, who must have been very dear to his poor parents. Mother said that Aunt Bessie was fond of telling one story about Thomas Isaac, recalling the occasion when he was asked to say grace before breakfast one morning and steadfastly refused although commanded several times by his father. When asked several times for an explanation he eventually said very plaintively, 'Daddy, you don't say grace for porridge!' It was considered by the family to be a very amusing incident.

He was only about four when he died and I think it was totally unexpected, because I believe that the doctor who had tended him had remarked previously that he wished his own son, who was about the same age as Thomas Isaac, had been as robust. His death was not due to any lack of care because they owned their own house and were reasonably well off. It was just one of those tragic quirks of fate.

His father was very proud of his house because he had built it on a bit of land at Low Fields and did quite a lot of the construction work himself, with the help of his bachelor brother, Tommy. I know that when it was finished, he turned to his wife and announced triumphantly: 'There, Bessie. Now you can bide in your own house.' That was another oft-told story in our family because it must have meant a lot in those days, owning your own house instead of paying rent to a landlord.

So Mother filled the gap in their lives. It was a good home but both Richard, who was a bearded gentleman, and Bessie were rather strict. Mother told me that once when she had gone with them to chapel – and she was only a tot – she had just a little peep around at the rest of the congregation. Immediately a hand was placed firmly over her head and turned it to face the front again. The hand, of course, belonged to her great-uncle and foster father. Unfortunately, he did not live very long. His brother, Tommy, came to live in the house but he didn't survive very long either. There was so much sadness, so many funerals in my mother's childhood. Anyway, Aunt Bessie brought her up in the little house built by her husband and brother-in-law which was near to South Stainmore. And, just over the hill at North Stainmore, at Dummah Hill, Great-Uncle Isaac Bayles was looking after Daddy, and training him to be a farmer.

There is no doubt that both had hard lives. Mother served her time as a dressmaker with a maiden lady who had a business in Kirkby Stephen and made a bit of money that way. But she also had to keep house for Aunt Bessie and for a lodger she had to take in to make ends meet. He was a schoolteacher and a very nice man, I understand, but there wasn't much opportunity for Mother to go out and have a little enjoyment and apparently Aunt Bessie did not encourage such things. She had a sister who was much more understanding. Mother called her Aunt Mary, and thought she was a grand woman. She had children of her own, you see, and would try and persuade Aunt Bessie to be a little less strict with Mother. 'Let her be', she would say. 'Let her have a bit of enjoyment.'

Then Aunt Bessie had a stroke, more than one in fact, and burned herself rather badly, because she apparently suffered one when she was bending down to tend the fire. That meant Mother had to quit her dressmaking career since Aunt Bessie couldn't be left alone afterwards. Of course, that created an extra burden. I don't know how she managed to find the time, but when she got older she also played the organ for the Sunday services at the local Methodist chapel, as well as running the choir practices.

It may have been at the chapel that Father began to court Mother. She never really said. But they would have met when both the Tallentire brothers became ill and died and something had to be done about the farming land that went with Aunt Bessie's house at Low Fields. Great-Uncle Isaac at Dummah Hill, where Father was living and working, was kin to the brothers so an arrangement was made for him to take over the land. Of course, that meant extra work for everyone at Dummah Hill, particularly Father. It wasn't an easy courtship because there was so little time to spare after the day's labour was over. In fact, with Daddy it was all work –

apparently he put in some ridiculous hours. He was so conscientious, and the conditions were not good. Uncle Tommy, his only brother, used to tell me, in jocular fashion, that the only difference between Daddy and himself was that Daddy went into work and he ran away from it. Grandmother used to say that if it had been possible to take their personalities and shake them together a bit it would have been better for both of them.

I still have some letters which Mother and Father wrote to each other – beautiful letters, which are a revelation of their lives, both when they were courting and after they were married. Mother, who was two or three years older, used to worry herself sick about the way he toiled, going on every hour sent in all weathers, and not stopping to change into dry

opposite, *Hannah's mother as a young woman*

below, *Hannah's father as a young man*

clothes when the weather was wet. They could only snatch a few minutes together from time to time, usually when Daddy came over to Low Fields to look after the cattle, or during the haytiming.

In time, they decided to get married and Mother made her own wedding dress from a roll of silk given to her by her mother. I still have it. The wedding was held in 1920 at Mouthlock Methodist Chapel, at South Stainmore, where Mother was the organist and, much to her surprise and delight, the members of the chapel presented them with an inscribed silver teapot. It became a great treasure because there wasn't much money to spare in those days. But it was solid silver – and the inscription must have cost a bit as well. I keep it safely tucked away.

It was a nice wedding, necessarily modest. Uncle Tommy was Daddy's best man and Mother's sister, Violet, was the bridesmaid. Grandad Tallentire gave away the bride and I think Grandad Hauxwell performed one of his well-known recitations. I do believe they wore top hats, but there are none of the usual wedding photographs to confirm that. Daddy thought that photography would be too expensive and Mother declared that she wasn't bothered. I can't imagine how, given their circumstances, but they did manage to afford a week's honeymoon by the sea in Morecombe. A whole week to themselves. Mother said they stayed at a nice place, a boarding house I believe, and apparently it was a special experience.

But then they had to come back and resume their lives. She housekeeping for Aunt Bessie and the lodger in South Stainmore, and he farming over at North Stainmore. They could not live together. That's probably why they had to write to each other even after they were married. It was to be more than five years before they were able to lead a normal married life. They would spend the occasional weekend together when the chance occurred, but that's all.

Nowadays, people wouldn't put up with those circum-stances, but in those days it was accepted as a fact of life. They had to face reality and did not pine for what was not possible –

just got on with life as best they could. I know Mother used to help out at Low Fields in an attempt to ease Daddy's burden a bit.

Mother stayed with Aunt Bessie until she died. That was a bad time for her because she fell between two stools in a way. She lost her home, was apart from her own family and my father, and did not fare very well at all when the time came to divide Aunt Bessie's property. I do not think she benefited at all financially – if she did it was a very small amount – and wouldn't have been able to keep any of the furniture had it not been for the kindness of Aunt Mary. The kitchen table I have today came from Aunt Bessie, along with my rocking chair, a brass pan and some pictures. Aunt Mary made sure that Mother left with something.

It was Aunt Bessie's death, coupled with another event, which did finally bring Mother and Father together permanently. You see, Great-Uncle Isaac at Dummah Hill had a housekeeper called Eleanor Anne Cleasby and she and Uncle Tommy got married, which caused a bit of a mix-up. By that time, Uncle Tommy was living at Sleetburn in Baldersdale with his parents, my Grandfather James and Grandma Elizabeth Hauxwell, and his new wife didn't want to leave Dummah Hill. So the family agreed on a swap – Uncle Tommy would go there and Father would take over Sleetburn, which was rented from a man called William Hutchinson.

But even the happiness Mother and Father felt at being able to live together under the same roof at last was tinged with sadness, because they both liked Stainmore very much and would have preferred to stay in the area. And then they couldn't be on their own because they had the elderly relatives to care for. Of course, fate decreed that they never would.

Life at Sleetburn created other problems for Mother. She had never farmed before, and she told me that it did not come easy. I think she was twenty-eight when she learned to milk, and she said it made her knees shake.

I was born at Sleetburn, on 1 August 1926. Mother and Father had been married for six years and I was to be their only child. Dr Dawson, a wonderful man who died not long ago,

was present and my arrival had an unfortunate repercussion. Maybe it was a difficult birth – no one ever said – but Mother got up too soon because there was a lot of washing to do and contracted pleurisy. Father had to poultice her, which is what they did in those days.

I cannot recall anything about Sleetburn. My earliest memories are of Low Birk Hatt, which Daddy bought at auction when I was three, at what turned out to be an inflated price. Paying off the mortgage created difficulties when the income from the farm declined during the bad times, which was more often than not, when prices fell for our sheep, cattle and produce.

I can remember as a small child Daddy coming back from Barnard Castle with big loads on his bicycle. And there was an occasion when we were at a chapel anniversary service and Mother had to go on the platform to sing. She had a lovely contralto voice. I didn't take kindly to being parted from her and climbed up beside her.

The Depression happened when I was little, with the Jarrow march and all that dreadful unemployment and suffering. I was oblivious to it all, but I don't know how we managed, as agriculture suffered along with every other industry.

Daddy was the only able-bodied man on our farm. The elderly relatives did what they could but it meant that all through his life – not that he even survived to forty – there was never a chance to take it a bit easier, no one he could rely on to do the work if he was ill or tired. And Mother had her hands full coping with the housework and looking after four old people.

In addition to Father's parents, two bachelor uncles came to live with us at Low Birk Hatt: Great-Uncle Isaac from Dummah Hill and his younger brother, Great-Uncle William Bayles. They all became ill and infirm, which increased Mother's workload, and it was all made worse because of the lack of space. Low Birk Hatt has three bedrooms but the back

opposite, *Eleanor Anne (née Cleasby), wife of Uncle Tommy Hauxwell. (The flowers in the hat are believed to be real!)*

bedroom wasn't used very much because it had no fireplace and couldn't be heated. So Grandma and Grandad had one bedroom, Mother, Father and me slept in the other one, and the two brothers slept downstairs.

I know Mother worried a lot about the money situation, but Daddy kept a tight control on things and people in Baldersdale were very good at helping each other out. The bank was usually very understanding, and generally gave us some leeway until we were able to sell something. And a firm run by Ralph Willie Raynes, which used to supply most of our goods, would allow extended credit when it became necessary.

The pity of it was, not long after my father died in 1933 things improved quite a lot in the material sense. A grand little chap called Willie Workman was largely responsible. He lived over in Westmorland and was in the milk business, and then he met and married a Baldersdale girl, Anne Coldfield from Dill House, and they came to live here. They took over the farm at Blind Beck and Willie pioneered the collection of milk throughout the whole dale. Up until then people had made butter and sometimes cheese from the milk since there had never been a collection until Willie, who was a very good businessman, began to transport it out – on a horse and cart at first, until he acquired a wagon. It led to a vast improvement for everybody in Baldersdale because it provided a regular income. Making butter was nowhere near as reliable.

Then war broke out in 1939 and made a difference, as it always does. Farm prices inevitably improve at times like that, which is sad in one way, but it removed a lot of worries in Baldersdale. We were given subsidies on cattle and sheep as well. I don't remember hearing Mr Chamberlain announcing the outbreak of war, although we had a wireless by then. We were probably all busy out in the fields at the time since it happened at the beginning of September. The news got around, I believe, when somebody went and rang up a newspaper, probably the *Darlington and Stockton Times*, to enquire. By and large, the war passed us by in Baldersdale, although we had to go through the business of putting black- out curtains at all the windows, even though all the light we had was from oil lamps.

Nelly (seated) and Lizzie Hauxwell, Uncle Tommy's twin daughters

I think maybe half a dozen men went to war from Baldersdale, and poor Sidney Fawcett from West Birk Hatt was shot and killed while trying to escape from a prisoner-of-war camp. Sometimes I would hear conversations about the war when some of the older men in the dale came to chat and have a cup of tea in the kitchen with Uncle Tommy, who had come to take over Low Birk Hatt after Father died. Unfortunately, his marriage had broken down and he and his wife had separated. They had three children – twin girls, Lizzie and Nellie, and a son, Willie.

Uncle was quite keen on listening to the nine o'clock news and I remember hearing Mr Churchill. We got our ration books – for us and the cattle-food as well – but I don't think I ever worried about the possibility of Hitler invading us. The war was so far away and I suppose it was only in later years we learned how serious the threat was. We had other matters on our minds at the time, as it happens. Grandma Hauxwell died in December 1940, and that left just Mother, Uncle and myself. Grandad was dead by then and so were the two great-uncles. There had been rather a lot of funerals at Low Birk Hatt and they weren't inexpensive. That tended to balance out the extra income from the milk collection and the wartime subsidies, so we never really achieved the desirable state of feeling well off.

The only gunfire we heard was from the army rifle range across the hill, and sometimes they would bring tanks up on big wagons so they could practice on the moor.

The biggest excitement of the war for us happened when an aeroplane came down on the hill above Clove Lodge, which is just across the valley from Low Birk Hatt. But it was one of ours. I don't know what sort of plane it was because it was unrecognizable. It ploughed into the ground scattering debris and bits of aluminium all over the place. Friends took me up to have a closer look at it, and I understand the pilot, who was an Australian, managed to bale out and came down safely somewhere near Balder Head.

The war brought a lot of changes to Baldersdale, however. At the start, work was done by horsepower in the strict sense of the word. Then the first jeep, war surplus, came into the dale and it was cut down to turn it into more of a wagon. It was followed by the first tractors, the little grey Fergusons. They were grand machines. But Low Birk Hatt was never able to support such a luxury.

5

Bikes, Circuses… and the Wonders of the Wireless

The twentieth century arrived rather late in Baldersdale. Some corners missed part of it altogether, none more so than Low Birk Hatt. Even during the last decade before the dawn of the twenty-first century, the prospect of water on tap there was still problematical. When Hannah was a child, running water meant the stream in the field and such things as electricity, the internal combustion engine and even the wireless were available only on another planet, or so it must have seemed to the average resident of this remote and lovely, but intensely deprived valley. As she grew up, a few of these technological marvels began to slowly percolate into the Dales. Personal transport had since the dawn of time been limited to footslogging or a horse not too exhausted by its labour in the fields. But the bicycle arrived, and then the two wheels driven by a mysterious force, known as a motorbike. Far more significant and revelatory was the arrival of the wireless, in the sense that it meant for the first time the voice of the outside world and all that it encompassed – good and bad – was heard throughout this enclosed community. It encouraged Baldersdale to look up and beyond its natural boundaries. The days of innocence were over – well, almost.

We got our first wireless second-hand from John Thwaites at High Birk Hatt just before the outbreak of war in 1939. I think it cost thirty shillings. It was a Pye and a grand set it was too. John helped us to fix it, setting up the outside aerial with those little white pot things with holes in. They resembled the pot eggs you used to put under hens to encourage them to lay.

It was run on accumulator batteries which were filled with acid, and they were the big drawback. They lasted all too shortly – maybe a fortnight or so – before they needed to be recharged, and they always seemed to fade at a crucial time, in the middle of your favourite programme. But Mrs Fawcett at

West Birk Hatt had a brother, a clever man called Tommy Rayne, who could charge them. Trouble was he lived at Selsit, which was up over the Pennine Way, across the high moor, and it meant a three-hour trek there and back. Those batteries were big, heavy glass things and took some carrying, particularly on a hot day. Fortunately, we had friends at Kelton, which was on the way, about an hour's walk into the journey, so one could stop and rest. There were risks involved because the acid sometimes leaked and I ruined a couple of dresses that way. One was a very nice garment made out of a kind of silk which Mother and I bought from the secondhand clothes lady who ran a stall in Barnard Castle. Mother used some washing soda to try and get the stain out but it didn't work. I still have the dress, which only goes to prove once again how difficult I find it to throw anything away!

When we arrived at Selsit, we would exchange the flat battery for a fully charged one and walk back. The charge was sixpence – six old pence – which is 2½p today.

The wireless made such a difference to our lives. We felt less cut off from society as a whole and I was particularly pleased to be able to listen to good music on a regular basis.

Eventually we got another wireless, a Murphy I think, again second-hand, from John Thwaites. It would have been wonderful if we could have been able to afford a gramophone as well. I know Mother would have liked it because she had some experience of one when she was living with Aunt Bessie, over in Stainmore. When she was young, Aunt Bessie had been in service for a well-off family with a certain Mrs Leigh, who lived in Colne in Lancashire. Aunt Bessie used to go and stay there and take Mother along too. The Leighs worked in a cotton mill and they had a gramophone, which Mother thought was a wonderful thing. But then you couldn't just switch it on and listen to the music like the wireless. It was necessary to buy records, and that factor would have put it beyond our reach. Such a pity.

But for Uncle Tommy, I think an even bigger thrill than the arrival of the wireless was the day he acquired a motorbike. He bought it from a chap called John Dowson, who later married one of the Miss Sayers from West New Houses. I believe the sum of fifty shillings (£2.50) changed hands.

It was an Imperial and he was so proud of it, although he sometimes had considerable difficulty in making it go.

Neddy Fawcett, who was farming at West Birk Hatt in the days before it was flooded when the new reservoir opened, was very good with mechanical things and used to come over and try to make it start.

I would sometimes ride on the back to go to chapel, or shopping, and the furthest I ever went was when Uncle Tommy took me to Middleton in Teesdale to see Sir Robert Fossett's Circus. I was about ten at the time and I found it all a bit frightening. I had never seen such crowds before and when we joined the big queue to get in, some of the young people became 'up by' as we say, which means excitable. A lot of pushing and shoving went on and I panicked a bit, so Uncle picked me up in his arms to protect me and calm me down.

opposite, *Neddy (Edmund) Fawcett with wife, Meggie, and daughter, Margaret*

below, *West Birk Hatt, the remains of which are now under Baldersdale's top reservoir*

My memory of the occasion is rather vague otherwise – perhaps it was obliterated by the fear I felt. I do recall a pal of Uncle's, called Will Rayne, who was dressed in a check suit, struggling out of the crowd and sitting down somewhat red in the face from his exertions, on the tubs in the ring before the performance started. And I do believe there were some elephants, which I liked. But I can't recall much else.

The next circus I attended, still before the war started, was Bertram Mills at Darlington. Now, that was a much more orderly occasion with people waiting patiently to enter the tent instead of creating a crush. We didn't go on the motorbike that time, since Darlington was rather a long way and the general unreliability of the machine argued against using it. We walked down to Cotherstone, caught the bus and stayed the night with our relatives in Piercebridge.

An even bigger treat happened during the war when we went to Darlington again to see Big Bill Campbell and his Rocky Mountain Rhythm at the Hippodrome Theatre. Now, we never missed Big Bill's programme on the BBC if we could help it – it was just so tuneful. They were all there, including Buck Douglas and the Old Log Cabin, and the theatre was absolutely full. It was exhilarating because they were just as good in the flesh as they were on the wireless.

By that time poor Uncle had no motorbike. It was just a brief spell of ownership; the war meant petrol rationing. He did love it so. Today, when I see people on marvellous new motorbikes, just flying about and knocking them to bits, it makes me feel so sad. If he had been able to ride one of those he would have thought he was a millionaire.

I had two wheels of my own as it happens – still have, in fact. My first bike was a Hercules, which Grandma got for me from a niece of hers. Uncle tried to teach me to ride it but I didn't really become proficient because I was scared of falling off, and the area around Low Birk Hatt wasn't much good for cycling.

I never rode around bends or up steep hills. I would get off and push. Now I did once ride it to Cotherstone Show around the time I was twenty-one and going there was just fine because it was mostly downhill. But a neighbour kindly brought it back to Baldersdale for me. I think that was the last time I had a proper ride on a bike. Other traffic on the road always worried me, so I would stop and get off until the way was clear. Years later when I saw John Sayers of West New Houses for the last time before he unfortunately died, I mentioned that I was planning to start riding my bike again, and he was most amused. He knew that I had always stopped and got off if there was anything else on the road – and that was back in wartime remember – so he said that with the sort of traffic that's on the road now I would never be on for getting off!

Later on in life I did acquire another bike, a Raleigh, and a good, stout little bike it is. It was all due to the kindness of a lady, Miss Margaret Higginson, who became one of my dearest friends. She was the headmistress of a school in Bolton and read about me when Alec Donaldson wrote an article in the *Yorkshire Post*, which was the first time my name was brought to the attention of the public. Then some of her pupils walked the Pennine Way, which runs through the land around Low Birk Hatt, and she sent a message and a box of chocolates with them. Now, I am sadly lacking when it comes to corresponding, but that time I did manage to write and thank her, adding that she would always be welcome to come and call if she ever was in the area. I didn't expect her to do so, but what I didn't know then was that she had a holiday cottage in Muker, which is not far over the hills in Swaledale, and one day she turned up with some friends of hers.

By then, I hadn't got a wireless but she declared that it was an absolutely necessary thing for someone in my situation and brought me a red one, of the kind that worked on batteries – thankfully, not the kind you had to carry for miles to be recharged! And when that one 'went home' she provided me with another one, which is still going today.

One day she turned up with the Raleigh bike because she was worried that I didn't get out much. That was twenty years ago. It was some years before I actually tried to ride it, and that was all because of the kindness of Martin from Sunderland. I

The Hippodrome in Parkgate, Darlington, a generation ago
(Courtesy of Darlington Library)

am afraid I don't know his second name, but I have been his friend since he was a boy. His family used to come and stay for a week every year in a cottage across the dale and Martin would come and visit me on a regular basis. He was such a nice boy. He had a dog and, being city-bred, he thought Baldersdale was wonderful. A real place of adventure. I've seen Martin grow up. One year he arrived with a young lady, then came back when she was his wife. Then they turned up with their little son, Daniel, to introduce him to me. I suppose he will be nearly grown up now.

Well, one year when he was about seventeen, Martin arrived to sort out my bicycle. The Raleigh. I hadn't ridden one since just after the war. He oiled it, pumped up the tyres and held it for me while I had a go, just in the yard at first. Then I tried it on the pasture, but that was a bit rough, so I thought I would ride it down the new road through the iron gate leading out of my land. It has a fairly pronounced slope and a hump in the middle which proved my undoing. Twice I came off at that spot.

The experience rather put me off but I still have the Raleigh with me in Cotherstone, and keep hoping to have another go. But if I do, I will have to keep to the by-roads, because the traffic on the main road outside my cottage can be very busy in summer.

We never had perils like that in Baldersdale, so civilization can have its drawbacks. Nevertheless, I do admit relishing its other benefits, particularly water on tap. A water supply was very slow coming to Baldersdale and never did arrive at Low Birk Hatt. The only place I know which had water supplied by the Tees Valley Water Board was West Friar House, which was owned by Roy Bainbridge. Apparently, he had reserved certain rights which entitled him to a supply. Other people had to get their water from where they could, and at their own expense. Some were more fortunate than others because their land had a spring.

There was a plan once to supply our place and the Fawcetts' at West Birk Hatt from a source within the boundaries of High Birk Hatt, but the Fawcetts had to leave when their farm disappeared under the waters of Balderhead Reservoir which, ironically, put paid to that enterprise.

Uncle was still alive – but not for long – when electricity came to Baldersdale around 1961. Now that was such a big thing and caused a lot of excitement. A few places further down the dale had got it at once, and then it began to advance further up towards us. The electricity people called to ask my permission to put poles in my land so that they could take it even higher, and I agreed to it. But I don't think I ever seriously considered having Low Birk Hatt connected when they offered it to me. It was the expense, you see. It just was not possible.

6

Leaping Preachers, Soporific Sermons and the Art of Muck Spreading

For more than a hundred years throughout the Dales of Yorkshire, the pivot of community life, the one platform for self-expression open to everyone, was the chapel. It had a virtual monopoly on social life, organizing the annual outings, sports days, tea parties and concerts which were the highlights of the year in an era which was starved of communication and leisure and wearied by the constant treadmill of work on the land. During Hannah's childhood and well beyond, Dalesfolk lived in a closed world where to travel more than a dozen miles from the farmstead was an unusual adventure, the wireless a strange and suspicious device from foreign parts and a local newspaper something of an occasional luxury.

The less formalized form of religion brought to the Dales by John Wesley and his brother suited the collective personality of these people perfectly. For a long time there had been a struggle for supremacy between the established church, the Quakers, the Catholics and the Congregationalists. The spiritual history of Cotherstone reflects the ebb and flow of religious influence in the Teesdale area. George Fox arrived there in 1653 and established the Quakers as the dominant force in the village. The next village just down the road, Lartington, stayed loyal to the Church of Rome, which led to a spot of tension now and then. The Church of England established their place of worship in 1796, then built St Cuthbert's in 1881 and a school in 1894. The Congregationalists arrived in 1869, but the balance of power shifted to the Methodists around 1874. They, too, added a school to their chapel and the Wesleyan message spread swiftly into the more remote corners – the far-flung network of small and isolated communities like Baldersdale.

The heat of battle has died away now. Both the Methodist and Church of England schools in Cotherstone have been replaced by a state school (the Methodists hung on until 1960). But it is still generally recognized as a Methodist village, and Hannah is counted among the worshippers at the chapel who are, in the main, elderly. But when Hannah was a girl, chapel was a place for the young and energetic, for people who wanted their voices to be heard. Life in those days offered few opportunities for young men and women with ambition. But one way of making your mark was to become a preacher.

My goodness, we certainly did have some outstandingly good preachers around these parts, particularly before the war. Sometimes, whole families of them, like the Beadles of Upper Teesdale who were familiar faces in Methodist pulpits. There were three brothers, Jacob, Phillip and John, who were very much their own men and who would stick to a viewpoint through thick and thin. They were marvellous speakers, even though I understand they did not have the benefit of what was considered an education.

Rather strenuous debates on religious issues were quite commonplace and Uncle Tommy was always ready to take part. He knew the Beadles well – they were very forceful and witty and Uncle would have many a fierce but friendly argument with them. I think maybe he didn't share some of their more extreme views.

Mind, Uncle could be just as witty as them sometimes. There was one occasion when he was in discussion with Jacob Beadle, a very strong, good-looking man, and the topic was muck spreading. In those days, the manure was distributed on the fields in heaps from a horse and cart and then you would have to follow behind with a handfork to rake it and spread it evenly. It's a task I am well familiar with myself.

Anyway, Jacob said that he could do the job better and more quickly if he paced himself by singing a lively hymn called 'Keep in Step with the Master'. Uncle replied that Jacob's choice was no good for him. His own particular selection for the job was the much slower 'Art Thou Weary, Art Thou Languid'!

Uncle did some preaching too, in and around the Teesdale area, but I never went to hear him. It would have been embarrassing for me. I did listen to him proposing a vote of

A parade of Methodist preachers active in Teesdale, taken in 1948

Uncle Tommy in later years – centre, with white hair, glasses and left hand on chin

thanks occasionally, and I was always glad when he sat down.

Some of the preachers used to be very enthusiastic, not to say a trifle over-active, when delivering their message. Uncle used to tell the story about one of the fiery kind, a real character, who delivered a sermon one Sunday in a chapel with an unusually long pulpit. As the sermon wore on and he became more and more excited, he began to jump from one side, first to the middle and, by the time he was in full verbal flight, he managed to leap the entire length of the pulpit. The congregation was mesmerized.

I have vivid memories of several preachers who came to

Baldersdale, particularly one evangelist called Rhoda Dent. It was quite unusual in those days for a woman to become a preacher, but she was very good and most eloquent. She came from a family that lived on North Stainmore, where my father was raised, and she had striking looks. She was well built, with strong features, and she styled her dark brown hair in what they called earphones. You needed to have a good, full, thick crop of hair to plait in order to achieve this effect, and I thought it nice.

On one occasion she held a mission at the Methodist chapel in Baldersdale which went on every night for two weeks. People came from many other local chapels to attend, which meant quite an effort in those days when very few people had cars. People mostly walked or came on bicycles. Some of those services used to build up a wonderful feeling, and now and then it would become rather emotional with the preacher calling on folk to come forward to the penitents' bench at the front to re-dedicate their lives to the Lord.

Rhoda Annie Dent was her full name and I understand she was once invited to speak on the *Queen Mary* during one voyage. In later years she went to Leeds and married a minister. She kindly wrote me a letter after the first television programme about me, since her family and mine had been friends for years. Her father, Ralph Dent, a somewhat excitable fellow, was a pal of Uncle's and they used to have many animated discussions about different aspects of religion. Rhoda had a brother called Tom, a very pleasant ·young man who also became a preacher, but not for long because, unfortunately, he died young.

Another preacher who made an impression locally was an Irishman called John Wesley Kingston. He once held a mission in Romaldkirk which I attended. He was a fairly good-looking young man and I do believe he came on the recommendation of Rhoda. He wrote a book which we bought, all about the discrimination he endured as a Methodist living in Ireland.

Personally, I didn't care a lot at all for the more dramatic kind of preachers, those who would shout and thump the

John Wesley Kingston, Irish evangelist

opposite, *Rhoda Dent, taken c. 1930*

pulpit. It is perfectly possible to get your message across without being so histrionic. And those sermons, they did carry on so. It was particularly hard to bear when one was a child. You would think that they were – thankfully – drawing to a close, and then they would burst off again for another hour and you found yourself wishing they would just shut up.

I know that nowadays the congregations at chapels have sadly declined but if the services lasted as long today as they did in my childhood they would be empty altogether.

Some of those involved had quite a critical, holier-than-thou approach. I recall one occasion when Mother was so busy trying to finish knitting a quilt – I've still got it somewhere – that she said she would have to miss a service. They were having a mission at the time and the preacher told Mother that it would have done her far more good to go to chapel than knit a quilt. Mother wasn't moved at all.

Uncle used to tell me about the time when the Primitive Methodists and the Wesley Methodists were joining up. This created a lot of controversy and gave those who were fond of the sound of their own voices an unrivalled opportunity. They used to have what they called 'quarterly meetings', where the various stewards would render reports and accounts. They were always verbal marathons. No, those long-winded gentlemen put me off sermons for a good long while. And then, of course, I wasn't able to attend much when I was left on my own after Mother and Uncle Tommy died and I had all the milking and farmwork to do myself.

When Grandmother was alive, I would go to the church services held in the schoolroom in Baldersdale because Grandma was Church of England. Mother used to come too, although she was chapel, and then we would go on to the Methodist service in the evening. Although I was baptized into the Methodist faith I used to prefer the church service because it didn't go on so long. Mind, I do worry about the Church of England because of its beginnings and its association with Henry VIII. He is not a character I like at all because I think he was just an old rascal. You hear about the times of good King Hal, and the rather implausible suggestion that he wrote 'Greensleeves', but I don't see him in any romantic light at all. I am just glad I wasn't Anne Boleyn, or some other lady who took his fancy.

Now, as far as the Catholics are concerned, I have to say I like the people very much but theirs is not a faith I could accept myself. I know things have altered recently, but certainly at one time you couldn't speak to God yourself and confess your sins direct to Him. You had to do it through a priest. Neither am I happy about the ceremony and the burning of incense. Then there is the question of the nuns and monks entering one or other of the orders where they become prisoners, more or less. To me that seems intolerable. I know people have written saying that I look like a nun, or could have been a nun, but that's the last thing I would want to be. Life must be free to do what one wishes and, to a certain point, to say what one wishes. To have to do what someone else says, and to be behind bolted doors is just unacceptable to me.

The reason I prefer the Methodist faith is because it has the simplest form. They also have the best hymns, good old jolly tunes. I can be far more moved by music than any sermon. I mean, take Beethoven's 'Pastoral' Symphony. If there is anything capable of lifting you up to the gates of heaven, then that is it.

Now, I must stress that Christianity is very important to me, although maybe I am not deeply religious or believe enough. One hopes there is a heaven where one will meet up with one's loved ones but I don't know. That's why I look upon death as a horrible thing – it seems so final. We don't know what's on the other side, if anything. I just cannot blindly believe that we move out of this life and enter into a better one.

Nor do I believe that to be a good Christian you have to attend chapel or church every week, or even three times a year. The most important thing is how people live. There are a lot of good people who may never enter a place of worship. But I do go to the Methodist Chapel in Cotherstone as often as I can and, now and again, support various chapel functions in other places when asked. I even made an appearance at a big Salvation Army event in Sheffield one weekend.

And I have met the man who is probably the best-known preacher in the world today, Dr Billy Graham. He was a guest on the first *Wogan* show I appeared on. We stood together in the entrance hall of the theatre where the show is produced, but I have to confess that I didn't recognize him. Later, we met very briefly. We couldn't talk because I believe he badly wanted to telephone someone who had just returned from China, so it was just a handshake really. Not a conversation, but a very good handshake. Still, I liked him, and I have heard him on television once or twice. And when you think he is in his seventies and working so hard night after night, you have to admire him.

Not long after meeting him I went on a bus trip to a rally

Billy Graham on the Wogan *show* (Courtesy of Russ Busby)

held in a big place where they had an enormous screen with Billy Graham appearing by satellite. There were such a lot of people there. In fact, it was full – which I didn't like very much because I am nervous in crowds. But the organ music was lovely, although some of the vocalists sang rather modern stuff, a bit like rock and roll. I'm not so keen on that but I know that they have to attract young people as well.

Dr Graham was, as you might expect, most eloquent and, when he appealed for people to come forward and dedicate themselves, quite a few got up and went towards the screen just as though he was really there. Of course, there were people positioned to receive them.

But I didn't go. In fact the room was so warm, and I have this tired feeling such a lot these days, that I'm afraid I fell asleep!

7

The Gentry: Beating for Grouse and the 'Slavery' of the Hiring Fair

Baldersdale was far too remote for any of the gentry to be interested in building a country residence there. All the more accessible dales had their halls, manors and castles, but the high moors sweeping up to 1,500 feet above the valley of Baldersdale was the habitat of a creature which every aristocrat, and many wealthy merchants and other *nouveau riche* with aristocratic pretentions pursued, then and now, with fanatical zeal – *Lagopus scoticus*, feathered-footed member of the Tetraonidae family, otherwise known as the red grouse. For the locals it meant an extra cash crop during the days following the Glorious Twelfth – the shillings and sovereigns tossed, somewhat disdainfully, at them for providing a back-up service, such as beating the heather to alarm the birds into the air and towards the buckshot, or placing their horses and wagons at the disposal of their lordships so that ammunition, lunch and the essential bottles of whisky could be transported to the guns and the day's bag of slain birds brought safely to the all-important count. For centuries the continual struggle of ordinary country-folk to harvest an income to keep them and their families above starvation level meant that they were always prepared to swallow their pride and go, cap in hand, to the gentry for a few vital coppers. The same philosophy spawned the hiring fairs (which continued until the second half of the century) when the 'spare' children of rural (and sometimes urban) families, not required for work at home, were sent to stand at appointed places where prospective employers could examine and inter-rogate them, checking their limbs for strength and making sure they were properly subservient. There wasn't a deal of dif-ference, fundamentally, between hiring fairs (as immortalized by Thomas Hardy in *Far From the Madding Crowd*) and the weekly cattle auctions held in market towns.

Hannah, and some of her friends in Baldersdale, have vivid recollections of the gentry and their ways, and personal experience of accepting the 'God's Penny' and going into service.

Leading Business Men Of The West Riding.

Sir Emmanuel Hoyle, of Huddersfield. Governing director of Joseph Hoyle and Son, Ltd., Prospect Mills, Longwood, Huddersfield. Four years, ago, more out of sentiment than anything else, purchased Portland Mills, Lindley, where his father, the late Mr. Joseph Hoyle, the founder, first began business. Is a firm believer in the idea that a principal can be his own best traveller, and has made several long voyages on business, on one of which he visited 27 countries and got orders in many of them. A fine type of sportsman, Sir Emmanuel has been prominently interested in the Turf, aviation, shooting, athletics, and football, as well as motor-racing. For some years was president of the Huddersfield C. and A.C.; now president of the Huddersfield Town Club. Past-president also of the Northern Counties' Athletic Association, was Northern Representative on the A.A.A., and has often acted as a judge and referee. Well known as an owner on the Turf, one of the first in this country to own a private aeroplane, and winner of many road-racing and hill-climbing contests. Some years ago became Conservative candidate for Darwen, but retired before the election owing to ill-health. Became a Knight of the British Empire shortly after the war, was knighted in 1922, and made a justice of the peace for the borough of Huddersfield in November, 1920.

Sir Emmanuel Hoyle, Master of mill and moor

Sir Emmanuel Hoyle owned the shooting rights in these parts. He came from Yorkshire, I believe, where he owned a mill and he could be quite a difficult man. I never met him and, after what I heard about him, I never had any ambition so to do. Uncle Tommy, along with the Fawcetts and John Thwaites from High Birk Hatt, used to work for him during the grouse season. They were nice takings you see, a bit extra, which was very welcome.

Uncle rented out our horse and cart to carry the lunch-baskets and the cartridges and to collect the bag at the end of the day. He said you could always tell first thing what sort of mood Sir Emmanuel was in. If he said 'Good morning, men!' as he passed by then it might not be such a bad day. But if he went stomping by without saying anything it was a clear indication of trouble ahead. Apparently, on one occasion, as he stormed past Uncle and Sam Fawcett, Uncle told Sam that someone was sure to cop it before the day was out. And it turned out to be them.

Sir Emmanuel had a florid complexion which, apparently, became redder and redder as his temper grew worse, and his language was appalling. Sam's brother, Neddy, incurred his wrath one day as he was driving the birds down towards the guns. He was the official gamekeeper and knew the job inside out but for some reason what he was doing didn't suit Sir Emmanuel and the air turned blue. And there was a bonny pantomime once when a couple of grouse went missing and Uncle and Sam got into trouble. They had been so busy collecting the birds and tying them up. Completely innocent they were, too, but it made no difference.

Still, Sir Emmanuel had the money. He was paying the piper.

The Thwaites at High Birk Hatt farmed alongside the Hauxwells, and John Thwaites worked with Uncle Tommy and the Fawcetts for Sir Emmanuel. John and his wife Marie live in retirement nowadays not far from Cotherstone and they actually cut short their honeymoon in order not to miss the shoot.

Aye, but you must remember that money was so scarce in the thirties that you couldn't miss anything. Marie and me were on our honeymoon, staying with my brother in Darlington, when I got this letter from my mother saying we must come back immediately because they were starting the shoot. You see, I had just graduated to the position of providing a horse and cart, and any amount of people wanted that job so I would have lost it, maybe for good, if I hadn't turned up.

The pay was fifteen shillings a day then, and that was for the horse, cart and man. An ordinary beater got five shillings. That was a lot of money in those days and there were a lot of men eager to do it – around twenty or thirty out of Baldersdale were hired. The shoot used to last five or six days in August but you didn't get paid when it was finished – don't ask me why, but we had to wait until Christmas. Later on, I believe, the pay went up to a pound or even twenty-five shillings for a man, horse and cart.

So we came back from honeymoon three or four days early. But Marie understood. My job was to take the cart up on the moor to a place called Mile End, and you sat with it all day until they brought the grouse to you.

Sir Emmanuel had a terrible bad temper and was often full of whisky. Most of his guests drank a lot, including some of the younger gentlemen. I particularly remember old Hoyle's solicitor, a great fat, brewsy fella from Leeds who drank whisky like a duck. And you had to be very careful with the grouse. When I first started on the shoot, Sam Fawcett said that I needn't bother about the whisky and the cartridges but I had to watch the grouse, and not to let anyone come past them and pick one or two out. Losing a grouse was the sin of sins. I never did lose any at all, but a couple did go missing one day and there was hell to pay.

George Fawcett, one of Sam's sons and now in his seventies, also has keen recall of his boyhood days working as a beater under his father's orders. Sir Emmanuel, as the owner of West Birk Hatt, was the Fawcetts' landlord.

Sir Emmanuel's men – the beaters and loaders from Baldersdale

The first drive I went on made me wonder about the sanity of grouse. The guns were blazing away at them but they just kept coming. Any other bird would have flown the other way. They could see their pals being shot down in front of them but it made no difference. They were daft birds, stupid. And some of Sir Emmanuel's guests were a bit that way, too. You were only supposed to take the birds directly before you, not follow them sideways because that meant the man in the next butt could come within range. Several times they ended up shooting each other. One day, an American guest became a bit too enthusiastic, aimed all over the place and ended up peppering several others, I believe. Father got it more than once over the years. One pellet lodged between his eyes and became a permanent dimple.

Sir Emmanuel was a fair shot and, on a good day, there would be three or four hundred brace to bring back. Once, the count topped five hundred brace – one thousand birds – but that was an exceptional day.

All the grouse used to be brought to my dad, who was awful particular about displaying them. We had a large table and Dad would lay them out in rows to cool, tuck their heads under their wings and put pieces of heather in between them. Damaged birds would be sewn up by Mother and their feathers ruffled to look nice. At the end of the day, they would all be taken down to Romaldkirk and put on a train, although on one occasion Sir Emmanuel had his private aeroplane sent up to transport them.

Mother used to make a big meal to feed the beaters when they came to unload and help pack the grouse, but the food for the gentry was taken to the moor in large hampers. They had a wooden hut built up there especially to have their lunch in, and there would be plenty to drink, including a hogshead of beer.

I know they are supposed to be a delicacy but none of our family liked to eat grouse. Some of the older birds could be very tough. Mahogany Joes, we used to call them, and there was a sure method of finding out if a grouse was getting on a bit. You put a bit of pressure on its mandible, or lower beak, and if it broke it was a young bird. If it didn't, it was a Mahogany Joe. Sir Emmanuel once sent us some grouse from his own table but it was not to our taste – it had been cooked in port wine and laced with some spices.

Sir Emmanuel was not an easy man to work for and you had to watch what you said. If any of the beaters did incur his wrath, they were sent home. One day a lad called Stanley Wallace created a real stir. I think he had been listening to some people in the dale who had missed out on the shoot and the money that went with it, and were critical, or pretended to be critical, of people who worked for Sir Emmanuel and the other toffs – maybe a bit left wing, although Stanley wasn't a person who took any interest in politics. Anyway, he was standing near to Sir Emmanuel, who was shooting from his butt, and a bird went down in front of the guns. Sir Emmanuel told him to go and pick it up, but Stanley replied, 'Go and pick it up yourself!' That caused a tirade, naturally, and instructions were given that the man must not be hired again.

The other event that I remember well was when my Uncle Ned could have made himself a bit of money when a bird was shot down in mistake for a grouse. Sir Emmanuel asked Uncle Ned what it was and he said it was a young cuckoo. But Sir Emmanuel was certain it was a hawk of some kind and offered to bet Uncle Ned fifty pounds that it wasn't a cuckoo. The bird was sent off to be identified by a taxidermist and Uncle turned out to be right. Unfortunately, he had refused to take the bet since it was a heck of a lot of money in those days, was fifty quid. But Sir Emmanuel was good in other ways and he used to buy our wool at a fair price. A solicitor friend of his who came on one of the shoots did a big favour for one of the beaters. He noticed that the man was missing one eye and asked him how he had lost it. The beater said it had happened years ago in a quarrying accident. The solicitor declared that he should get compensation for that, took his case on, and the man ended up with £250.

At the end of every shoot Sir Emmanuel would give a big dinner for the beaters at the Fox and Hounds in Cotherstone. It was always a good do. Hannah's grandfather, James

On the grouse moor – sorting the day's bag

Hauxwell, was invariably invited although he didn't take part in the drive. He came because he could recite poems, particularly Rudyard Kipling, and at great length. He could do one poem with sixty verses without pause, and Sir Emmanuel would listen and marvel at his ability.

Subservience was expected by all levels of employer, titled or otherwise, and Marie Thwaites was one of a number of young men and women who were packed off to a life which was not only unacceptable by today's standards, but hardly believable. Hannah Hauxwell met several who were in service in and around the Baldersdale area.

I used to see them when it was the custom for young folk to gather at Cotherstone village at weekends, to chat and meet their friends. Lads and lassies who were newly hired locally would be readily accepted when they turned up, looking for a bit of company and conversation. I well remember a young man who aroused special interest one weekend because he had been taken on at a place which had a certain reputation. When he was asked how he was getting on there he replied, 'Oh, it's like heaven.' Well, no one could make that out, but it transpired that the lad had a sense of humour. 'Yes,' he said. 'It's like the Bible says – there's no night there. We just work all the way through.'

Some people did expect an awful lot from those youngsters for the few shillings they paid them. There were no set hours, no union to look after their interests and they were lucky to get out on a Saturday or Sunday to go to the chapel, or on certain special occasions to the cinema. The lucky ones had bikes but most had to walk long distances to meet up with their friends. But at busy occasions such as haytime, they didn't get any time to themselves at all.

Not all places treated them roughly though. Over at East New Houses in Baldersdale the youngsters they hired were regarded as family. They had to pull their weight, but they brought up one or two who had lost their parents just as if they were their own children. They ended up getting married from East New Houses, with all the affection and ceremony you would give to your own child. My half-cousin Norman Bayles was hired over in Ravenstonedale and he liked it there. He was very interested in music and singing and would always be dashing off somewhere on his bicycle – later on, I believe he managed to acquire a motorbike – to practices and concerts.

The people at the farm he was hired to were very sympathetic but he still had all his work to do before he could get away. I know he was once asked to sing with a choir at the Kendal Festival of Music when Sir Adrian Boult appeared. But he had so much to do before he could leave, the milking and so on, and what with the long journey as well, he was very tired when he arrived and apparently nodded off. It seems Sir Adrian spotted him and shouted out: 'Oy – you at the back there! Wake up!'

Norman's music teacher badly wanted him to become a professional because he had a fine tenor voice and was a talented violinist. But there just wasn't the money available. Poor man, he died in 1989, just short of his eightieth birthday.

I know Marie Thwaites was in service at the time she was courting John. I liked her from the moment I met her, and I well recall the occasion – I had turned up at their place and she appeared in the yard from the shed carrying buckets of milk. Very cheerful and friendly she was then, and always has been.

Marie Thwaites has a sunny disposition, rarely stops smiling and has happy memories of her experiences as a hired hand. She considers herself one of the fortunate ones, although her innocent description of the daily regime she had to endure would be considered intolerable, indeed cruel, today. But the deprivation of her early childhood in the depressed North East does explain a lot.

I was brought up in a pit village near Bishop Auckland and I never knew my father. He was a miner and he went off to the First World War and got killed. I only knew my mother and grandmother and life was not easy – we often went hungry. When I was a schoolgirl some friends took me on to a farm and I used to watch the milking and think what a grand life it was, so healthy, not at all like life in the pits and the factories. By the time I was fourteen I couldn't wait to get away from that place and my mother took me to the hiring fair in the marketplace in Bishop Auckland. The year was 1931 and there were a lot of other lads and lassies standing around anxiously like me. All the farmers stood apart in groups, looking around. Anyway, this man came up to where I was standing with my mother, and asked if I was for hire. I said yes, that I wanted a farm place, and he asked me if I had any experience. I told him that I had watched cows being milked – that was all – but I liked the look of it. He must have liked the look of me because after a bit more discussion he said, 'Well, we'll have to learn you to milk, and learn you to feed calves and the rest will follow on. Here's your God's Penny'. Then he gave me half a crown. I nearly fell through the floor because I didn't know what owning such a lot of money was like before.

He was called Walter Dowson and a real gentleman he was. And his wife was a real lady. They had such nice manners and treated me like one of their own, so I reckon I was one of the lucky ones. Their farm, West Park, was in Lunedale and I travelled by train to Middleton in Teesdale. I was a bit lost because I had never been anywhere before, but I was met in a pony and trap and taken to my new employer. And I found I had a room all to myself. They had two children, a girl of five and a boy of two, and one of my first jobs was to take the little girl to school.

The week started at around six on a Monday morning – washday. First, I would clean the fireside, get the fire going, put a clean cloth on the table and lay it for breakfast. Next, I

Mr and Mrs Walter Dowson

had to get the cows in although there was usually a hired lad to help, and start the milking. I couldn't do that properly at first, but Mr Dowson came to show me how, telling me to pull a lot harder. The calves were to feed then, and the milk put through the separator to take the cream off. Back in the house I would start the housework until Mrs Dowson served the breakfast at around 8.30 a.m. She usually cooked bacon in the oven and there was an egg apiece, fresh from the hens on the farm. Well, I had never tasted anything so good in all my life!

After the breakfast things had been washed up I had to take the milk separator to bits and wash each part and dry them in front of the fire and then put them together again ready for the night's milking. The main housework followed, and all the oilcloth floors had to be scrubbed – houses that had oilcloth in those days were supposed to be well off. The only carpet was in the best room, or the visitors' room as they called it.

We had roast meat once a week on Sundays, served at noon on the dot, usually their own home-killed sheep or pork. It would have to last cold for most of the week, with a bit of bacon in between. But every day we would have a pudding, rice or suet, and always different.

The Dowsons' place was known as a good meat shop. I knew of one farm where they served the suet and gravy first so as to take the edge off their hunger and save the meat.

On Monday afternoons there was the ironing to do and, on other days, the cleaning and scrubbing. There were no detergents or soap powders, just washing soda that came in pellets and was used for everything, including the floors and the clothes. Then we had to grind best white sandstone to powder and scour all the top surfaces, including the ceilings. That stuff made everything beautiful. We used a tin of powder, a damp cloth and plenty of energy.

After tea at 4.00 p.m. – usually apple pie – there was the milking to do again and then we would settle down to patching, mending and darning, and making rug mats. Every year we would have to finish two mats. Well, there wasn't much else to do in the evening until one day Mr Dowson arrived and said to me and Mrs Dowson: 'Now then, I've got

In service – Marie Thwaites, aged seventeen

something for you lassies', and brought in a wireless set. It was great. The year, I think, was 1936.

They paid me five shillings a week, which was a lot more than most got. I heard the story of a lad, from the Bishop Auckland area like me, who worked at a farm in Teesdale for two shillings and sixpence a week. But the time came when he reached the age when the farmer had to pay sixpence a week for his insurance stamp, and he was sent back home because the man said he couldn't afford it. After a while, the lad turned up back at the farm and offered to work for two shillings and pay his own insurance stamp. When he'd arrived home there had been nothing to eat and not even a bed of his own. That's how it was for lots of families in those days.

Anyway, I had enough to save up to buy a Raleigh bike – one pound it cost – which meant I could cycle over to Middleton in Teesdale on my night off. There was a little shop there run by a Mr Nixon who would stay open all hours for the hired lads and lassies. The best part was his clog-repair service. I always wore clogs, and if an iron came off while I was cycling to town I could take it to him, go off somewhere like the pictures, and it would be ready and waiting for me straight afterwards. And he only charged sixpence. He also stocked bulbs and batteries for bike lamps, all kinds of useful things.

I will always maintain that I had a good time in service, and from what I heard there weren't many bad places in the Teesdale area – just the odd one here and there. But they said that it was a different matter over in the west, around Appleby way, where they generally paid more money but worked you very hard and gave you little meat. They told some awful stories about going hungry, no privileges, putting the fire out at six o'clock at night. In winter it got so cold that you would have to wear your clothes in bed.

No, I was well treated, although the hours were long.

I just got Saturday and Sunday nights off, and it would be chapel on a Sunday of course. There was a general rule that lads could stay out until ten o'clock on their night off, but lassies had to be back at 9.30 p.m. Before I got my bike that was a problem, because there was a distance of three miles from Middleton in Teesdale to the farm. You could get an extension, if you asked permission, on Saturday nights for a special occasion such as a dance, and then I met John at the carnival in Middleton. The bike came in very handy then because it's about nine miles to Cotherstone, where we used to meet.

Once or twice a year I would go home for a weekend to see my mother. I even got a job for one of my half-sisters at a place in Lunedale, but she didn't settle to the job like me and wanted to go home after a short while. But another sister followed me at the Dowsons when I left to get married.

After the wedding I came to live in Baldersdale, at the next farm to Hannah. We got on well from the moment we met and we still see each other from time to time, and talk for hours about the good old days.

8

Adder's Tongue, Moonwort and Frog Orchid: the Legacy of the Hauxwells

In the summer of 1987 a curious figure could be seen roaming the upper reaches of Baldersdale, dressed in wet-weather gear, festooned with notebooks, large-scale maps and a magnifying glass, and peering intensely over the dry-stone walls. Clearly not your average Pennine Way walker, he was, in fact, a botanist called Mike Prosser, who had been contracted by the Nature Conservancy Council to survey the area for species of rare plants and flowers which are known to flourish in certain areas of Teesdale – given the right, exceedingly rare conditions. He fell into a lively discussion with one of Hannah's neighbours which was the precursor of an important ecological event. Mike Prosser vividly recalls the occasion.

The gentleman in question did exhibit a certain alarm because when I told him why I was looking at his land he thought it might lead to a conservation order being slapped on it. He urged me to look elsewhere – particularly in the fields owned by an old lady at the next farm called Low Birk Hatt, because they were far more colourful than his. So I did as he suggested and began to walk through her land towards the farmhouse. As I walked and as I looked, I experienced what birdwatchers call a 'jizz', the feeling they get when they spot something very out of the ordinary. You could call it the Eureka factor. Certainly, I knew I had found something special.

I have to admit I had never heard of Hannah Hauxwell – well, you see, I do not possess a television set. I found her by the side of the house with her dog, looking like a complete tramp, with a patched-up old coat and hair all over the place. I had been told she was a trifle eccentric, and there she was, busily washing scores and scores of empty jam jars in two buckets of water. She was obviously the only person around, so I introduced myself and told her what my mission was. At first, I did most of the talking, and I remember asking her

250

name, which she said was Hannah Hauxwell. When I enquired if it was Miss or Mrs Hauxwell, she said, 'Oh no, no, no – Miss by name and Miss by nature, that's what my uncle always said'. Then she gradually took over the conversation, talking about her parents and the farm, saying she knew she was old-fashioned and some people laughed at the way she farmed, but she was happy with her methods and she liked the animals. Inside the farmhouse, she showed me some of her furniture and when I saw all the cards around the place and she began to talk about how proud she was about the large number of people who wrote to her, it dawned on me that she must be a bit of a celebrity. I thought she might have been the subject of a newspaper article or something like that, but it wasn't until later that I found out just how famous she was. She was quite happy to let me do my survey and eventually I had to make my excuses or she would have gone on chatting all day.

Hannah also recalls this meeting, which was to have a most satisfying outcome. She was surprised to learn that her meadows contained so much of ecological value and was somewhat confused at first when Mike Prosser turned up that day.

I had what I refer to as the Flower Gentleman come to call on me – I'm terrible at remembering names – and I liked him at once. It came as a surprise to learn that my pasture was so interesting to him, and I should be ashamed, being a countrywoman, of being so ignorant about the plant-life around here. I used to look at things and think how bonny some of the wild flowers were – what nice colours – but I was never aware of their variety or rarity. When I was a child there was a damp place in the long meadow where there used to be a lovely yellow flower we call butterballs, and children would bring them for the teacher. There was one I used to pick in another field years ago, a purple flower with pretty leaves which sometimes turned all colours, but I never knew its name.

I suppose such things were happy on our land because we never put chemical fertilizers on it. When we got the Hill Farm

Subsidy and we were obliged to spend a certain part of it in putting something back in the soil, uncle liked Middleton Lime, so he spread a bit of that around along with basic slag, and cow manure, of course. All natural things. But I didn't do anything like that after Uncle died in 1961, so that means my land has had nothing but cow manure for twenty-five years.

So it was all a happy accident really.

I did notice, however, that some of the wild plants and flowers that seemed to do well on my pastures didn't grow in other people's fields. Mind, I have always appreciated wild-life, even if I was unaware of the names or importance in the ecological sense, and it was also apparent that our farm attracted some lovely butterflies, particularly on warm days.

I used to enjoy the bird-life, too. Some very pretty specimens used to come into our garden and perch on the windowsills but I don't know what kind of birds they were. I've seen a heron standing on one leg, and I particularly liked the owls which used to shout from our trees to their friends across the valley at Clove Lodge. I even met one in the walnut tree when I was working in the garden one night.

I am delighted at the result of the Flower Gentleman's visit.

The Flower Gentleman in question, after setting about his detailed survey following that memorable first meeting with Hannah, quickly brought in a team from the Nature Conservancy Council to confirm his findings. The Durham Wildlife Trust was alerted and their bid for the main portion of Hannah's pastures won the day. An appeal for £25,000 was launched and the money came in so rapidly that the fund was over-subscribed within a couple of months. The World Wildlife Fund chipped in with a generous sum, and one lady donated £4,000. It is more than likely that the association with Hannah Hauxwell has something to do with the spectacular success of the appeal. The fields will be named after her, and a suitably inscribed plaque installed.

But no one has more reason to feel satisfaction at the turn of events than the quiet and modest Flower Gentleman, Mike Prosser.

It took less than ten minutes to register how rich and distinctive Hannah's land was – possibly the least improved meadows in upland Durham in fact. And by 'least improved' I mean untouched by artificial fertilizers or reseeding. Also, it had certainly not been ploughed this century, if at all.

There are some special aspects to the ecological makeup of the Teesdale area unknown elsewhere, which are rooted in the ice age. There is no simple explanation, but there are two main threads. Firstly, the altitude and harsh weather in the winter meant Teesdale was not good for tree regeneration, so it is one of the few areas in England and Wales which never became deeply forested. It has remained a type of upland grass area since the recovery of vegetation after the last ice age, ten or eleven thousand years ago. The other strand concerns the local geological history. Whereas fairly large areas in the Yorkshire Dales and up to the Scottish Borders were not heavily forested, the Teesdale region had this peculiar sugar limestone, creating a very thin, calcium-rich soil which never produced dense grass cover. But other plants were allowed to develop because the unusual chemical composition of the soil did not allow aggressive species to take over. This led to an enormous diversity of plants, none of them doing particularly well and none taken out by trees. Once you get a fertile soil, the bully boys tend to take over and only about half a dozen plants flourish. So Teesdale has a tremendously rich flora – indeed, some people think that many of the species are ice-age relics, which were there before and managed to hang on. The seeds of some of them may be millions of years old.

For these plants to survive, even in these beneficial conditions, it is necessary to have traditionally managed hay meadows. They were once very common in Teesdale and its tributary dales, like Baldersdale, but with the coming of intensive farming the picture changed dramatically. There was increased reseeding and cutting for silage, which entails heavy fertilization of the grass so that it grows very quickly to give you an early crop, then putting in more fertilizer to enable you to cut it again. Sometimes it is possible to get three crops a year, an enormous yield. But that also means that wild flowers and herbs get cut before they have a chance to flower and propagate.

The old way was to graze the fields over winter, then, somewhere at the beginning of April, take out the cattle and let the grass grow. In the higher dales haymaking was sometimes delayed, for weather and other reasons, until the middle of July or even towards the end of August.

I understand that Miss Hauxwell usually didn't cut her grass until well into August, so that gave the plants plenty of time to bloom and seed. And there was only one cut a year. The old way of farming.

So that was what I was doing in Baldersdale – looking for survivors in what has long been known to be a botanically rich area. One glance at Hannah's meadows told me that it had very real prospects because it did not have the lush, emerald green appearance of chemically fertilized land. It was a thin, washed out, yellowy green – just the kind of grass to excite a botanist. And it certainly turned out to be of considerable scientific interest.

There were dozens of species, including lady's mantle which has a very delicate green-and-yellow flower, and in certain varieties grows nowhere else in Britain. Another rare one was adder's tongue, a fern growing four inches above the ground with rather fleshy, pale green, diamond-shaped leaves. From the base of the leaf a spike appears, bearing two lots of bobbles containing thousands of fern spores. But the percentage of germination is very low, which was another reason for its poor survival prospects. An even rarer plant doing nicely on Hannah's land was a relative of the adder's tongue, the moonwort, which has a similar structure, but is a bit more complicated. I have no idea why it has come to bear that name.

Then there was the frog orchid which was not a rare plant until its kind of habitat became rare, and the eyebright, a pale little semiparasitical flower which twines into the roots of grasses to take nourishment. It has a whole range of colours, from all white, to white with blue, purple or mauve spots.

The cuckoo flower was there too, a lovely pale pink or pastel mauve which was one of the commonest wild flowers in Britain fifty years ago, but in another fifty years may be difficult to find. And what I thought was the prettiest sight in Hannah's meadows was the *Geranium sylvaticum*, or hay sward, which is a beautiful blue with a tinge of violet. When it's growing wild and bold, these flowers give a spangled mauve colour to a field.

Yellow is also a dominant colour in Hannah's meadows, but closer examination reveals the bright blue of the harebell, the crimson of the ragged robin and many other delicate shades.

Altogether, Hannah's meadows constitute a very rare and beautiful piece of land which will now, thankfully, be preserved for ever and farmed always in the Hauxwell manner.

The complete list of plants and grasses surviving on Hannah's land reads like a poem. They include meadow foxdale, downy oatgrass, crested dog's-tail, wood horse-tail, red fescue, sweet vernal grass, wood anemone, bugle, wood crane's-bill, globeflower, floating sweetgrass and sharp-flowered rush.

The Durham Wildlife Trust has set up permanent areas for study, and a completely detailed survey of the flora and fauna has been started. Although the special nature of the flora has been established, little is known yet of the fauna and it is considered that the insect and invertebrate community will be equally fascinating.

Hannah outside her new home, Belle Vue Cottage, Cotherstone

above, *The main bedroom*

below, *'I'm like a child when it comes to running water'*

above, *Hannah's new friend, the telephone. It's an ex-directory number or it would never rest*

below, *The mail continues to pour in, from more than one continent*

above, *An afternoon chat with friends, Mrs Annie Bousfield and Mrs Hannah Iceston, on the village green*

below, *Hair like spun silk, backlit outside one of the village pubs*

above, *Off to collect her pension at Cotherstone Post Office*

below, *Checking the prices in the window of Kelvin Walker's shop*

above, *A classic Teesdale hay meadow*

below, *The 'Flower Man', Mike Prosser, relaxing by a stream*

Adder's-tongue fern
(Ophioglossum vulgatum)

Moonwort (Botrychium lunaria)

Frog orchid (Coeloglossum viricle)

Geranium sylvaticum

Lady's mantle (Alchemilla)

The 'Hannah Hauxwell' Rose

In 1989 Hannah achieved a long-held ambition when a new friend, Mrs Nancy Smith, who has a farm in Stokesley, took her to Stokesley Show – an event which usually merits two full pages of text and pictures in the *Darlington Times and Echo* which are always read with deep interest by Hannah, who loves flowers, particularly roses.

Exhibiting at the Show was a rose-grower called Eric Stainthorpe, who had 'invented' a new rose – quite by accident. He had been cultivating a strain of 'Sweet Dreams', the variety which had been selected as the Rose of the Year in 1988. One day he noticed that a mutation of this rose, pink in colour, had emerged naturally, and he set to work to make sure it did not revert – and succeeded. The rose was still unnamed when he was introduced to Hannah at Stokesley Show. 'Oddly enough,' says Mr Stainthorpe, 'I had three names in mind: "Herriot Country", "Hadrian's Wall", or "Hannah Hauxwell". I have long been an admirer of Hannah, and I have read the books and seen the television programmes. But when I met her and shook her hand I had a feeling which is hard to explain – other people have had the same experience when meeting this lady. I felt so very humble. I knew immediately what I wanted to call the rose, and asked her there and then. She was obviously pleased to accept and I presented her with a basket of roses to celebrate.'

The 'Hannah Hauxwell' rose is a shell-pink patio rose and was officially launched at the Gateshead Show in the summer of 1990. Hannah was the guest of honour and presented the prizes.

9

Cotherstone's Hidden Gastronomic Tradition – and the Salty Secret of Mrs Birkett's Success

The village of Cotherstone, situated four miles northwest of the market town of Barnard Castle, was an early target of the fledgeling tourist industry, since it was within easy charabanc reach of the conurbation of Darlington, Durham and even Newcastle upon Tyne. Day-trippers and weekend visitors have filled the streets and riverside paths every summer for more than sixty years, but only a tiny percentage are aware of the village's remarkable gastronomic distinction, about which most communities would continually drum up a publicity fanfare.

Cotherstone cheese has been discreetly celebrated for well over a century. *White's Directory* of 1840 ends its brief thirteen-line description by declaring: 'Cotherston [sic] is noted for the manufacture of cheese of the same form and quality as Stilton cheese'.

To be bracketed with Stilton, the very king of English cheeses, is praise indeed. And Cotherstone cheese is made to this day, as keen readers of the *Good Food Guide* will confirm, and is available for sale at Cotherstone's post office. Superb it is too, with a long list of discerning enthusiasts ordering it regularly. It is featured proudly on the cheeseboards of several temples of gastronomy, and richly deserves much wider acclaim.

There is a simple reason for its relative anonymity. As far as can be ascertained, the future of Cotherstone cheese appears to be in the hands of one lady. And she refuses absolutely to communicate with the media. Many feature and food writers from various newspapers and magazines have tried over the years to obtain information and interviews and all have been denied. Her identity is widely known in the village, but her wishes are respected and her name will not be revealed here. She is the last of a long line of illustrious cheesemakers and her regular clients can only hope that she will pass on her expertise to the next generation.

Hannah knows her, of course, but she is as tight-lipped about names and places as everyone else in Cotherstone.

A little bit of secrecy does no harm now, does it? The existence of Cotherstone cheese is not widely known but that is the way the lady wants it, and those who like it can always find it.

Mother used to make cheese when she was young and she said there was an awful lot of work attached to it. We had a cheese press at Low Birk Hatt but I never recall it being used by our family. It stood outside in the garden for years until John and Vera Brittain took over from the Thwaites at High Birk Hatt. They came the year after the big storm in 1947 and she decided she would turn their spare milk into cheese. I don't think she had any experience but she became friendly with Eleanor Fawcett who had, and Vera borrowed our cheese press. She obviously learned quickly because she began to sell it quite successfully.

Vera would supply us with some from time to time and I know Uncle was partial to it. But I have never been a lover of cheese myself, except with Christmas cake.

There were several known cheesemakers in Cotherstone and the best known was a former Miss Chipchase, who married into the Birkett family at West Park Farm, which is situated along the top road into Baldersdale. I do believe people came from far away to buy her cheeses.

The sole surviving member of that family still lives in Cotherstone, just a few yards down the road from Hannah's cottage. Mrs Margaret Nixon was born in 1920, the youngest child of Mrs Katharine Birkett, undoubtedly Cotherstone's most famous cheesemaker. She was celebrated in the media, was featured in a 1940s radio programme and built up an impressive list of clients. Sacheverell Sitwell, the Marchioness of Bristol and the Countess of Rosebery, plus a clutch of other aristocrats placed regular orders, and a certain Mrs Demarest of the Manor House, Harrold, Bedfordshire, used to send twelve small cheeses in lieu of Christmas cards to a selection of her titled friends. The price varied from one shilling (five new pence) to one shilling and sixpence a pound, postage extra! Mrs Nixon still cherishes letters of appreciation from eminent people.

Mother's success was due in some part to her brother, my uncle, Charles Chipchase, who went to London in the 1920s and got into conversation with a newspaper reporter. He wrote an article and everyone started asking for our cheeses.

Mother was born into a Quaker family living at Lathbury, a hamlet near Cotherstone, went to a Society of Friends boarding school and later attended a course on dairy work run

Mrs Birkett, the famous cheesemaker of Cotherstone, busy at work with her daughters (Beamish, North of England Open Air Museum)

by the North Riding County Council at Helmsley. She used to visit local farms, struck up a friendship with my Aunt Hannah and was introduced to Father. They married in 1910 and she came to live at West Park, where Father was farming with his sister, Hannah.

There were quite a few noted cheesemakers in Cotherstone at the time, including the Misses Hutchinson and the Hodgson family, and Aunt Hannah also used to make cheeses with the help of my Aunt Mary, who lived in Lartington, and showed them at Eggleston Show.

It's generally accepted that the herbiage of this area produces the milk necessary to make a fine cheese. The richness and variety of plant life in Teesdale is well known, particularly in the lower-lying areas where some plants common in the south have their northernmost limit. That, together with certain northern species, and the legacy of limestone soil created in the ice age makes for our lush meadowland.

Naturally, Mother began to put into practice what she had learned at Helmsley. But she used a different technique to the others when it came to the salting. The really busy time was in the spring after the cows had calved and there was plenty of milk. The morning's milk was poured, still warm, into a large pan and set by the fire because the temperature had to be kept around 93°. We used a floating thermometer. Rennet – a piece of calf's innards usually – was added straight away. No other starter was used. You had to keep stirring all the time and, after an hour or so, the milk set solid and then was gently cut to allow the whey to flow out, leaving the curd. It was quite pleasant to eat at this stage – the curds and whey of the Little Miss Muffet nursery rhyme. The curd was then put into a straining cloth and left to drip with a blanket wrapped round it to keep it warm. At this stage, most of the cheesemakers – all the others perhaps – placed the curd into a vat of brine. But mother crumbled it up and sprinkled dry salt over it instead.

Then it was packed into various sizes of moulds from pint pots for quick unmatured sale, to the larger, more standard shapes and pressed with huge stone weights for twenty-four hours. Each cheese was wrapped in muslin bandages, placed

Mrs Birkett, straining the fresh, warm milk (1938/9)

opposite, *Breaking up the curd*

in a warm drying room and turned and rewrapped regularly.

Different grass at various times of the year used to produce different cheese. June milk was the best and strongest because you could leave it to turn blue for Christmas. We used to charge the top price for that – one shilling and sixpence a pound. A lot of our well-to-do customers liked it blue. I suppose it made a change from Stilton. I still have a letter dated September 1939, just after the outbreak of war, saying that 'Sir Fowler Harrison would be obliged if Mrs Birkett would supply eight or nine pounds of Cotherstone cheese, going blue if possible, and another ready for eating at once'.

left, *Putting the curd into the vats*; right, *Pressing the curd*

Later on you got what we call the fog cheese, from the second crop of grass in the autumn after haymaking, which was very rich but did not rise quite as well. And, do you know, before the war we could turn the cows out in the lane outside the farm before breakfast on summer mornings to graze the hedgerows because there was just no traffic at that time.

Weighing the finished cheeses

We delivered it locally from a pony and trap and I don't suppose we made all that much until they wrote about Mother in the London newspaper. Then everybody wanted it and she had to give up a bit of buttermaking she also did to cope with the demand. Some people used to call and insist on taking one away before she was really ready to sell it. Local shops even sold postcards of a photograph of our farm.

She also found the time to raise five children – Tommy, Bill, Jack, Molly and myself, the youngest. We all had to help in the dairy. My father died in 1927, when I was seven, but Mother carried on making cheese until around 1940. She died in 1952 and I am now the only one of the family left alive.

Delivery day – Willy and Molly Birkett

No one carried on the cheesemaking tradition in our family, although West Park Farm is still owned by the Birketts, run as a beef farm by my sister-in-law and her young son.

So these days I have to buy my cheese like everyone else. I have tried the Cotherstone cheese made today but I prefer something a little drier. So I get Wensleydale for myself and Cheddar for my husband.

10

Dogs, Country Remedies ...and the Cow with a Left Hook

Since Hannah lived in total isolation for more than twenty-five years, never married or even formed a relationship with a man, it is not surprising that most of the care and affection she had to offer was lavished on animals. She loved them all, each and every species to be found in the average Baldersdale farmyard, but was devoted particularly to dogs and cows. Suppressed maternalism it may be, but her passion shines through and she can recall in detail some animals, particularly dogs, that have been dead for half a century and some that didn't even belong to her. A fondness for dumb beasts may have been in the Hauxwell blood, because her Uncle Tommy, not a sentimental man in his later years, was a compassionate 'amateur' vet in Baldersdale. A good working dog – at least one – is essential for any stock farmer but the Hauxwells didn't always have much luck in finding the right one.

The first dog I recall from my childhood was little Meg. We got her from Sidney Fawcett, but she had a rather unfortunate weakness. She just could not resist rabbits. Now that's a real nuisance with a working dog because it doesn't matter where you have your beasts gathered or which direction you want to drive your sheep, a rabbit is always likely to pop up and Meg would be off like a shot. So Uncle arranged an exchange with our relatives at Piercebridge, and we got an Old English sheepdog, black all over, and called Roy. He was a lovely dog, but no good at working.

The next really special one was Peter. I had left school by then, and I was allowed to choose him myself from a litter. I called him Peter, after his father, who used to tour around a bit and always came to see me when he was on his travels. He was black with a smooth coat, and not a bad working dog. Uncle had a bitch called Jill at the time and they had puppies which we gave to the neighbours. Jill would work for me if

Uncle wasn't around but as soon as he appeared she didn't care a fig for me and would be off to see what he wanted to do.

But Peter was mine, and we had some grand times together, throwing sticks down by the reservoir. There were other dogs down the years, but the time came when I was on my own, and got a bit low financially, so I was not able to afford one. When your income is not much above five or six pounds a week, as it was for me in the seventies, even a tin of dog food is out of the question.

But one day, after that first programme, some friends from Halifax arrived with a little black and white Border collie pup, so small he could only just manage to get over the doorstep. He was called Chip and he stayed with me for around eight years. Now I have neither the patience nor the ability to train and discipline a dog, and Chip could be a bit wayward and excitable, but he was sometimes quite useful if you wanted to set cattle away across the field.

He had probably the nicest nature of any dog I ever owned, and possessed the loveliest eyes, brown in colour, and he was my dog definitely. When other people made a fuss of him, he hardly bothered with them, preferring to go over to wherever I might be and just sit there looking at me with those eyes.

Chip slept in a chair in the kitchen and was always at the door to greet me when I got up in the morning. If he wasn't waiting for me, I would know that something was wrong. You see, unfortunately, he didn't have a strong physique and eventually started to take fits. I had Mr Harris, the vet, out to him once or twice, and he gave him tablets which worked miracles for a time. But then he went into a bad fit and didn't come out of it.

I was so desolate about Chip. It's such a want when they have been there so long, that it's like losing a human being.

I should never have had the next one but I was in need of something. A rough-coated collie called Tip, he was offered to me by some relatives down the dale whilst I still had Chip. I refused him then but I weakened when they asked again after Chip had gone. Tip was a bonny dog, but a bully – even with me to begin with – and a real problem when the walkers came

Hannah with Chip

through my land along the Pennine Way. He would chase after them with me in hot pursuit, so he had to go back. Tip just wasn't my kind of dog at all.

In years gone by there had been some clever dogs in Baldersdale. The Fawcetts had one very intelligent sheepdog called Park, and the Sayers had one called Darkie, who had an unfortunate habit of being run over by farm vehicles. Then there was Rover of Clove Lodge, a large black dog who wasn't exactly a friendly animal.

I had another upset after the unfortunate experience with Chip and Tip. A dear friend of mine from Middlesbrough brought me a dog which turned out to have distemper, and he died. But then the same lady found Tim for me. He used to live in Thirsk but his mistress became too ill to look after him. He was almost two years old when he came to me.

I must confess I was a little disappointed when I first saw him, because he looked such a little old scrap after me being used to sheepdogs. But what I really liked was his face and we have been together for around five years.

He is very affectionate, and I wouldn't be without him now, and he has been to the vet's for his injections so as to avoid another disaster. A veterinary is what Uncle Tommy might have been if there had been the money to send him away to train, because he was very good with animals. People in Baldersdale often used to come for him to help calve their cows and, on one occasion, he worked alongside our local vet at that time, Mr Joe Cosgrove, who said afterwards he was pretty good. And professional people don't usually throw compliments around like that. Uncle once set the leg of a bull in Sleetburn, which must have been a tricky job, and I well remember the occasion when one of our cows had a really bad calving and Uncle saw her through. He had rheumatism and was known to be a bit quick-tempered and impatient, but even Mother remarked how surprised she was at his skill and patience when it came to doctoring animals.

There was another man, across the dale, called Ralph Tarn, who was also handy as an amateur vet. Of course, people would do as much as they could on their own, partly because

Hannah with Tim

it wasn't easy to send for a vet in a faraway place like Baldersdale, which didn't have many telephones, and partly because of the expense.

It was much the same when it came to doctors for the people. There were one or two ladies in Baldersdale who were very good at midwifery, which was just as well when a baby was on the way and the doctor couldn't get there in time, or the weather impeded him. And we had several of the old remedies at Low Birk Hatt, such as wintergreen and knitbone, and particularly aconite. Both Mother and Uncle were great believers in aconite, for either man or beast. It's a clear, almost colourless liquid in a little bottle with a spout on it, and Mother would put on her glasses and measure a drop or two very carefully into a drink for us, or into the water for the cattle. If you had a cold, aconite would stop it from developing, or keep a bad cold from becoming something worse.

Sheep we usually treated ourselves. I might still have the odd tin of some oval golden tablets, big as gooseberries, which we used to give them for worms. And on the occasions when there was an epidemic of sheep scab we all went to the sheep-dipping tub kept by the Fawcetts, and later the Thwaites at High Birk Hatt, to double dip them in a special drench. I didn't like that much because it was so smelly, but a necessary evil.

I was very fond of the sheep, especially when there were lambs, as well as the pigs and hens, but the dogs and the cows were very dear to me. When I was left on my own after the death of Uncle, my beasts became my family, I suppose. I couldn't let Rosa go when the time came to sell up. I know she is old and won't last forever, but she has been a good and loyal friend to me and I will stand by her.

A lot of people still remember Her Ladyship, the little white cow which was featured such a lot in *Too Long a Winter*, and so do I, of course. It was a very sad day when she became too old, ill and weak to carry on, but Rosa replaced her in my affections.

Her Ladyship was a mistake really. Her mother was much too young to have a calf but the gate got left open, or maybe the bull knocked it down, and she was conceived.

When I bought her as a young heifer, a friend went on and on about how small she was until I wondered if I was going to have a beast left at all by the time she had finished. But she turned out to be a grand cow, and a good mother to lots of calves. There were several bulls in the dale, but I cannot recall any serious incidents with them, although I know they can be very dangerous. We had one called Stumpy, a Dales short-horn, light roan in colour, which we reared from a calf. He had a nice temperament and you could go up to him and stroke him without fear. We had another one I really liked who shouldn't really have been passed by the Ministry man because his horns were too long. Nowadays, I believe all bulls have to be dehorned.

You couldn't keep bulls for long or the strain in your herd would have been weakened by in-breeding, so there was a regular turnover, and quite often farms would loan out their bulls around the Dales before selling them out of the area.

As a matter of fact, the animal that caused the most trouble – and some pain for me – was a little black heifer, a Galloway and shorthorn cross. All was well at first, but when she calved it was another story. She had a grand lot of milk, but she wouldn't let me milk her. The only way to succeed occasionally was to try when her calf was suckling her.

I had some real performances with that cow. She had a special, very unusual way of kicking. She could bring her milking-side foot round in a curve and very fast. It was a sort of left hook.

She caught me a couple of times, did that beastie. I called her Blackie – and a good few more things as well, I can tell you!

Sheep dipping with the Thwaites family of High Birk Hatt, c. 1930

11

Hannah's Successors: the New Owners of Low Birk Hatt

$$T$$he question of who would succeed Hannah Hauxwell at Low Birk Hatt aroused keen interest both locally and nationally. Hannah decided to divide her property, which spread over 78 acres of unforgiving land, into three parcels and invite sealed bids.

The house, together with 15 acres, was one of the parcels.

It was thought likely that some substantial Teesdale farmer might buy all three, ranch the land and sell off the house as a weekend cottage – a regrettably common practice which has been partially responsible for the steady depopulation of the Dales, particularly the more isolated places.

Many other permutations were possible but the future of the house did cause worry. There was even a rumour that the local authority was to acquire it and turn it into some kind of museum.

The hope was that whoever followed Hannah would respect the character of Low Birk Hatt and, to some extent, carry on the way of life of the Hauxwells and their kin, the only family to have previously lived there.

The outcome was – eventually – to be deeply satisfying to everyone who cherishes the ecology and traditions of this wild and beautiful place.

To begin with, the main pastures were bought by the Durham Wildlife Trust (see Chapter 8) and will be protected for all time. It has to be said that the prospects for the house and farm buildings did not seem promising when Gordon Pratt of Hawes Auction Mart opened the bids on 28 October 1988. The successful one was made by a couple totally unknown in Teesdale. Nor were they farmers. And total anonymity was demanded, so the waiting Press and television crews went away empty-handed.

They still want their identities to remain publicly un-announced. Their names and background are known to their neighbours in Baldersdale but they are very anxious to avoid as much as possible becoming involved in the publicity which continually surrounds Hannah and hope that interest in her former home will eventually decline and disappear. However, they have agreed to reveal their detailed plans for Low Birk Hatt and they are calculated to please the most critical defender of Dales traditions.

He is a successful business executive with all the trappings – heavy responsibilities, large car, mobile phone – and she also has a career, with professional qualifications. But both have their roots in the land and within a reasonably short space of time Low Birk Hatt is due to emerge, its amenities vastly improved, as a family home with cattle grazing the land around it.

Just as it always has been.

And he is quick to point out that it was a joint decision to make a serious bid.

Yes, we had both been searching for years for a place like this, well away from urban life with some land and outbuildings. We live about an hour's drive away from Baldersdale and every weekend we would scour the 'Property for Sale' columns of the local newspapers. When we saw Low Birk Hatt advertised in the *Darlington and Stockton Times*, we realized who it belonged to because we had seen the television programmes.

We did wonder if we would manage to find the place but we located it one wet Sunday afternoon. As we walked through the gate, Hannah popped out of the byre and asked us to wait until she had finished showing someone else round. Then she shut us in the byre – and we stayed there a long time!

She was most meticulous in her guided tour, opening every door. And as we drove away, we hadn't travelled down the road very far when my wife looked at me in a certain way . . . and I knew that she wanted Low Birk Hatt as much as me.

It is going to be a family home. We have two sons, one already away pursuing a career and the other about to take A levels. So we won't be tied down to schools very much longer. And I have a job which involves quite a lot of travel so I am not too restricted about where I live. Incidentally, both boys are enthusiastic about the place.

Hannah and her 'family'

The new owner of Low Birk Hatt digging out for the new road

We have a two-year plan, which I hope will not turn into a rolling two years! Then we aim to sell our present home and move in permanently. It's proving to be a strain, both financially and physically – since we are doing as much of the work ourselves as possible – and our friends were convinced for some time that we had gone mad!

The first major thing I did was to have a road laid from the top, rather a long way. I dug out some of the wet land and a local man put down a crushed stone track in four days, so we can now drive from the main road almost to the front door. It was done with the co-operation and permission of the Nature Conservancy Council so as to avoid ecological damage, and I would like to point out politely that it is a private road.

A septic tank has already been installed and I have a quotation – amounting to some thousands of pounds, I'm

Finished – the road to Low Birk Hatt

afraid – to drill for water. But it has to be done. Judging from geological surveys, they expect to have to go down to a depth of 45 metres before they find it. And they won't give any guarantees, although I understand they haven't failed up to now.

We have bought an Aga, and intend to have central heating, probably oil-fired, as well as open fires. Inside, the walls have been damp-proofed by injection and I have re-layed the stone floor flags myself. In the big front room the flags were as good as new – no wear at all – and Hannah told me it had only been used for funerals and pig-killings.

I knew that Hannah had experienced problems with rodents so I expected to find rat runs and nests underneath the flags, but only mice had been there. I have only seen two rats, and they were both outside the house and both dead. But I did discover where they had been coming in – through the stable and into the wall – and where they had resided when I pulled down the ceiling lathes in the dairy and a load of old nests and rat droppings fell on to my head.

The only wildlife problem has been created by the jackdaws trying to nest in the front-room chimney, so I have pushed up a chimney brush to discourage them. That chimney turned out to be the only delicate part of the building and scaffolding had to be erected so that it could be rebuilt. Of course, that job had to be done professionally – by a local man, because I am trying to use local contractors wherever possible.

A farmer friend of mine came to look the place over shortly after we bought it and he gave me some useful advice: that, whatever happened, we must enjoy doing the work. I tried to keep his words in the front of my mind, particularly during the bad times when we were clearing everything out and the dust and debris of a hundred years was falling into our eyes. But, now we are beginning to put things back, I am feeling a sense of achievement.

The outbuildings, like the byre and the barn, will have to wait until later. The roof of the barn concerns me because eventually it will fall in but I dare not start on it just yet – the house must take priority.

Some of our precious time spent at Low Birk Hatt is taken up by a steady stream of Hannah's admirers, making a pilgrimage to a place they know so well from the television programmes and books. Most of them are very courteous and we haven't minded them having a quick look round, but some are less welcome. I hope this public interest will eventually fade away, especially when we have moved in for good.

When we do so, I intend to carry on with my job, which has agricultural connections. My original career intention was to go into farm management and I went to agricultural college. I worked on farms for a while before I joined my present company, so I know how to handle a tractor!

His wife has even closer links with farming. She is the daughter of an arable farmer situated well south of Teesdale, in an area where both she and her husband were born and brought up. And,

Converting the stable at Low Birk Hatt

Rebuilding the 'delicate' chimney

remarkably, she has formed an affectionate bond with Rosa, Hannah's much loved senior cow, which for part of the year returns to her old pastures because Bill Purves, the neighbour who cares for Rosa, rents the grazing from the new owners.

Rosa really is an old dear. She comes up to the house and starts bellowing, and just will not stop until you give her a cuddle! I intend to keep cows when we move in, very much the same way as Hannah.

We both know about farming – we even met at a Young Farmers' dance! And the isolation at Low Birk Hatt will not worry me, even when my husband is away on business, because my father's place was even lonelier.

The prospect of winters here is something we will have to prepare for carefully. A four-wheel-drive vehicle will be an essential, of course, and my husband can leave his car at the top on the main road when snow is forecast.

The commitment which the new proprietors are bringing to the enormous task of totally renovating and modernizing Low Birk Hatt is patently obvious. For years they have denied themselves many of the luxuries they would otherwise have been easily able to afford because they both knew that one day they would need the capital to spend on the kind of home they both dreamed about. She even volunteered to do without an engagement ring, a classic case of long-term planning, if ever there was one.

Most weekends, they labour side by side to conserve funds for the jobs they cannot tackle. Their summer holidays are spent in the caravan they have positioned in the yard.

They have won the respect of their neighbours in Baldersdale, and even Hannah, although still psychologically adjusting herself to Low Birk Hatt belonging to someone else, is aware that her old family home is in good hands.

I liked them very much as soon as I met them, that very damp Sunday afternoon. And they were so patient as they waited for me to finish with my other visitors. I took them into the byre so that they could shelter from the rain.

Hannah with the new mistress of Low Birk Hatt

They were among a few people who came back to see over the property again quite a few times, and I met their sons. I talked to the lady for some time and we seemed to like the same things, so I was pleased when their bid was the successful one.

I did wonder at first whether or not they realized what they were taking on because Baldersdale is another world compared to what they have been accustomed to – very different indeed.

But it is good to know they have experience of farming and intend to make it a proper home and keep cattle. And I am very pleased she is kind to my poor Rosa – very pleased indeed.

When I handed over I did offer to come back and help, do a bit of walling for them, perhaps, but I didn't know then just how busy my life would be when I came to Cotherstone. I imagined I would have a lot of spare time, but my diary is always full.

Nor did I realize how difficult it would be to face up to going back. I'm frightened now that it will unsettle me, bring back too many memories.

But I am happy for them to be there and wish them well.

12

Meeting the Public...
the Wogan Shows...
and What the Papers Say

One of the many unusual facets of Hannah Hauxwell is her reaction to certain situations which would daunt much more apparently sophisticated people and which one would expect to be overwhelming for a simple soul from the back of beyond, such as meeting, on level terms, some of the famous and mighty, or appearing in front of milling crowds, and even standing up to address them.

But Miss Hannah Hauxwell is neither daunted nor overwhelmed. Whatever the grandeur of the situation, she transcends it with a sweet serenity which mesmerizes everyone. There have been many classic occasions down the years, one as far back as 1973 when the writer of this piece was a makeweight speaker at a *Yorkshire Post* literary lunch in Harrogate, attended by four hundred elegant people – mostly well-heeled, middle-aged ladies in all their finery. The heavily publicized leading speaker was an exceedingly famous television personality of the day, who shall remain nameless. Now, whenever this writer mentioned the name of Hannah Hauxwell, who was seated alongside him, he noticed a distinct ripple of excitement in the audience. So, as he concluded, he asked Hannah to stand up and just say 'hello' – that's all. To everyone's astonishment, she addressed the gathering with style and modest confidence for several minutes. The place exploded.

For the next two hours the literary lunchers surged around Hannah and virtually ignored the ostensible star of the show, who had been obliged to immediately follow Hannah and had fallen flat. He was not pleased.

Hannah never appears to be overawed by the great names. Whether it is royalty, legendary sportsmen or major politicians and broadcasters, she meets them all with much aplomb. More often than not, they turn out to be admirers, well versed in her background, and she finds herself answering the sort of urgent questions that 'normal people' ask when they are introduced to her: how is she settling to her new life?; does she miss Low Birk Hatt and her beasts?; is she taking care of herself?; and so on.

These days Hannah keeps an engagement diary. She is in constant demand to make public appearances and to give television and other media interviews. To accept them all would place an intolerable strain on her health, but she rarely fails to help a charity. She firmly refuses to concede that she is a celebrity, merely saying that she 'leads two lives' but is essentially an ordinary Daleswoman. But the effect she has whenever she does meet her devotees is startling. She has been known to stop the traffic on one of her book-signing sessions, a situation which eventually required the police to gently and good-humouredly sort it out. She has created records at most of the bookshops she has attended. On one December Saturday, Hannah sat in the Craven Herald Bookshop in Skipton and people queued through the premises, out of the door, down an alleyway and along the High Street. At any one time there were three hundred people patiently waiting in the most appalling weather. Many were there for more than three hours, but Hannah always gives full value for this kind of sacrifice, talking to each one for between five and fifteen minutes and writing in the book whatever message is asked for. There was a great deal of camaraderie in evidence and several promising friendships were forged in the crowd. Bookshop staff went round handing out sweets and, as the light faded, a portable telephone was taken along the line for those who wanted to tell their friends and relatives why they would be so late home. One woman walked for an hour through the snow to catch the bus to Skipton, waited for three and a half hours to meet Hannah, and still went home smiling.

Along with the hundred copies Hannah dealt with the following day for those who had been unable to reach Skipton, the staggering figure of five hundred books were signed. Many thousands more have been sold at bookshop appearances from the northeast to the Midlands, whilst at the Grove Bookshop in Ilkley, run by Andrew Sharp, *Seasons of My Life – the Story of a*

Book-signing session – a chat with an admirer

Solitary Daleswoman, is, by a huge margin, the most popular book ever stocked.

Television stations from Tyne Tees in the northeast, via Yorkshire Television (of course) in Leeds (the *Calendar* programme named Hannah 'Woman of the Decade') to TV-AM in London regularly ask her to appear in their studios, and often send film crews to Cotherstone. Without exception, the programme-makers depart gleefully with the material. Hannah always delivers – she is a natural communicator. Placing a camera in any situation usually diminishes it in some way, but the opposite is true of Hannah – the camera adores her.

Travelling the celebrity circuit has led to some fascinating encounters with certain household names including two sessions with the top talk-show man of his time, Terry Wogan.

Now, I must confess I hadn't seen much of Mr Wogan before I met him because, when I got my television set at Low Birk

Hatt, Richard Megstone, the nice young gentleman who looked after the Youth Hostel in Baldersdale and kindly took care of my electrical things, said I had a choice – either BBC1 or Channel 4. And I chose Channel 4. I recall hearing Mr Wogan on the wireless, but he was basically a stranger to me. So I went with an open mind.

I always enjoy going to London. It is our capital city, after all, and it is quite exciting to see the sights and stay in those lovely hotels – I like travelling by train too. Kathy Rooney, who worked with Barry Cockcroft for many years at Yorkshire Television, escorted me down on both occasions. This time in the hotels I particularly noticed how many people of different tongues were also staying there – all babbling away and making me wonder who they were and where they had come from. Quite fascinating! Some of the staff hailed from foreign parts too. I've had some interesting conversations with several of them, talking about opera with an Italian waiter, for instance. On another occasion, a lovely lady called Elsa who came to tidy my room, and who was from a South American country, took me into her confidence and told me about some of the problems she was facing. Quite a sad story really. And a gentleman who I think was Chinese had an accident with some plates whilst serving a meal, and finished up by giving me a kiss!

But those hotels are so big and confusing. I'm no good at getting into lifts and finding my room so someone always has to show me. The Kensington Hilton was enormous, quite the biggest place I have ever encountered to date. A person like me can easily get lost there – and I did! Kathy Rooney had to leave me one night when we were dining at the Kensington Hilton, so she took me to the porter to arrange for him to take me upstairs to my room when I was ready. But when I later tried to find my way back to the dining-room to finish my meal, which should have been a simple thing to do, I just could not locate it at all. Eventually I stopped a very helpful young lady member of the staff, told her of my predicament and she guided me back to my table.

I was very nervous when I went to meet Mr Wogan for the

first time but the gentleman who drove the big car to the show was very nice and friendly. He took me to the BBC Studios in Shepherd's Bush and I was introduced to the lady producer, who was charming. We stood a good few minutes in the entrance hall, and a gentleman came through and smiled, and someone said it was Billy Graham, Mr Wogan's other guest. But I wouldn't have recognized him. Then we went upstairs to the make-up room and Mr Wogan came to say a quick hello, which is his custom, I believe. But I wasn't there at the time. We did meet briefly in the doorway and I think he said something. I was a bit flustered at the time so I don't really know what he said.

I was given the opportunity to have a rehearsal with him but I declined because I am not like the professionals who can rehearse in detail and then put it over as fresh as a daisy when the time comes. So the first time I had a conversation with Mr Wogan was live on television!

Mind, I did rehearse the walk-on, which is quite critical. Kathy Rooney stood in for Mr Wogan, and I was a bit tense when it came to the real thing. But it seemed to go all right. I think they rather wanted me to wear my old farm clothes, but we compromised with a grey check skirt which a good friend gave me, and a blue jumper. I had been in television studios before but never with a live audience, so that was a bit different. After I got started and into the conversation I felt a lot more comfortable. I enjoyed talking to him, and thought him a very good interviewer – and that makes all the difference. After the programme we exchanged a few words, but he had to dash off to another engagement. Dr Billy Graham was also busy, and we met briefly in the doorway. I seemed to meet everyone in doorways that evening. But the lady producer and her researcher, Cathy Meade, were both very complimentary about me.

In fact they were clearly entranced by Hannah – which, it has to be said, is par for the course with everyone meeting this lady for the first time. Terry Wogan became so absorbed with her that he ran the interview into the closing music, leaving him scant time to promote his next programme – very unusual. The audience response was equally enthusiastic and Hannah was urgently requested to return to take part in *The Wogan Christmas Show*.

Oddly enough, I didn't happen to be in my room again when Terry Wogan came to see me before the show on the second occasion. Poor man – I don't know what he thought about me, but that's just the way it happened. And this time I didn't have to walk on because I was already installed on the sofa when the show began. Nor did we have a talk beforehand because he was on the stage doing a turn with somebody else – I think they call it a warm-up. There was an embarrassing moment when I thought he was walking over to me to begin the programme and I got up to greet him. But he called out, 'No, sit down, Hannah, sit down, we are not starting yet!'

That unsettled me a bit, but we eventually got going and it was all right. I have to say I enjoyed the first programme much more, simply because of the subject we had to discuss on the second one, which was Christmas. You see, I don't like Christmas very much because it brings back all those painful memories of the years when I was on my own and there wasn't much money – not much of anything at all. It is something inside me. I've had good Christmases since but it's a feeling I cannot shed. It's something, as I said on the programme, that I cannot be all starry-eyed and bushy-tailed about. So I was quite happy to sit back and let the other guests talk when they came on.

Afterwards, there was a little Christmas party in the entertainment room upstairs, and all the Wogan studio team came. Mr Wogan arrived and had a few words with me – and everybody else – but once again I don't recall what we talked about. The trouble is, I get all of a whirl at times like that. Mrs Wogan was there too. She was very nice and we exchanged a few pleasant words. Such a charming lady.

The Press has been conducting a romance with Hannah for nearly two decades. Reporters and feature writers wore a path through the pastures of Low Birk Hatt, and now they knock constantly on the door of Belle Vue Cottage, Cotherstone. Many miles of film have been exposed and several forests felled to supply the paper to print the wit and wisdom of Hannah Hauxwell. The British Press habitually looks for an opportunity eventually to knock down the heroes they have created and placed on pedestals, if only to do something new. Some writers probably set off with that idea in the back of their minds, but up to now Hannah has disarmed them all.

A perfect example of how Hannah emerges unscathed from the most penetrating analysis is contained in Alan Frank's well-constructed piece in *The Times* of January 1990. It begins:

'If you had not been told otherwise, you might think it was all a terrific affectation – this old woman from the Dales with the luminescent skin, the saintly set of the features and the clothes from the pile which even the rag-and-bone man would probably not take. . . . She has become what might be called The Professional Daleswoman.

It is enough to make you smell a rat and be damned for your cynicism.

Hannah Hauxwell is famous for being obscure, which by definition is a state of affairs that cannot last. She is one of those official curios so beloved by the British in their presentation of the living heritage – a Listed Person, withstanding the erosions of the impure present.

Yet if this extraordinary ordinary woman does get a private frisson of vanity from her fame then hers is a classy act of concealment. "I'm not a celebrity," she says with a levelness I was told to expect. "My assessment of myself is that I am a plain Daleswoman . . ." '

In the *Observer*, Janet Watts had no reservations: 'Hannah received me with the warmth and courtesy she radiates in the film and talked for three hours without any refreshment but a tooth-glass of tap water, in which she toasted my health.'

Byron Rogers, writing eloquently in the *Sunday Express Magazine*, was most concerned about the confusion of possessions Hannah had crammed into her new home:

'I offered advice. The room we sat in contained two television sets, two oak sideboards, slightly lower than the ceiling and four clocks all stopped at different times. "Miss Hauxwell," I said, "you'll have to throw something away."

Miss Hannah Hauxwell, dressed in men's trousers and old jacket so torn that it looked as though savaging by wolf packs had once been part of her daily routine, looked at me mildly. "I am no admirer of President Reagan," she said in her precise way. "But I must quote him here: You ain't seen nothing yet."

There was a mangle in one room rearing up out of the cardboard boxes like a stag, the chaos (or the wolves) had not yet pulled down. But it was a neat chaos of boxes piled on each other, cakes still in the tins they came in and hatboxes, one of which contained the last remaining ball of her long-ago childhood. In the passage, done up with string and still unopened, were the parcels and Christmas cards sent by the world and his brother when they learned she was moving home three months ago. . . !

Byron Rogers ended his lavishly illustrated piece with the words: 'This has been a late twentieth-century fable'.

Nancy Banks-Smith of the *Guardian*, consistently one of the best writers in journalism today, first wrote stylishly about Hannah in 1973, and in her review of the last film declared:

' "A Winter Too Many" was the elegaic end of a besieged life . . . the enthralling thing about Hannah, when Barry Cockcroft made that first documentary, "Too Long A Winter", was not the things she managed without: warmth, water, company, money. The world, I am pleased to say, is full of unreasonable old women. The thing about Hannah is Hannah herself.

Her voice was soft and low; her complexion a child's. She was so transparent that there seemed nothing but clear skin between what she felt and what she said. Something shone through. The effect was nunlike even to the headscarf which she wore indoors and out, like a wimple. This kind of shine, you felt, must come from a renunciation, not necessarily religious, of the world . . .'

295

But Miss Banks-Smith went on to worry about the effects of such overwhelming attention: 'You wonder with something like guilt whether television was good for her'. It *was* good to her. Viewers, touched by her life, sent gifts of money which she used to buy not comforts for herself but more cows, and that meant more crippling winter work. Well-wishers exerted a steady, gentle, concerned pressure on her to be sensible.

Financially, she was now as they say, quite warm. This Wordsworthian woman was transformed into a nice old lady in a cottage with a window through which to watch, as she said, 'the world go by'.

Most newspapers have simply reflected the public adulation: 'Unique Figure Fascinates Eleventh Telegraph Literary Luncheon' was the nine-column headline in the *Grimsby Evening Telegraph*: 'She was its star . . . she captivated the 330-strong audience with her simple charm'. One of the 'important' speakers was Tony Benn!

Another banner headline in the *Evening Gazette*, Middlesbrough, resulted from a tumultuous signing session, at Dresser's Bookshop in Darlington: 'Hannah, Oh Hannah! Magnificent Daleswoman'. The *Teesdale Mercury* ran 'Hannah Is The Star Attraction', whilst the *Darlington and Stockton Times* declared, after one of Hannah's appearances, that she 'received the sort of welcome normally reserved for royalty'.

13

Olive Field: the Lady of Lartington Hall

*T*oo *Long a Winter*, the film documentary which projected Hannah Hauxwell into her stellar position in the affections of the British public (and far beyond) wasn't really about Hannah at all. It actually told the story of an entire Teesdale community of which Hannah was just one member, albeit a 'lead' in the dramatic sense. But the viewers were blinkered. For them, no one else in the programme existed – except one. And since that happened to be another woman, she had to be remarkable – and she certainly was. Olive Julia Field was the lady in the Big House, Lartington Hall, just down the road from Hannah's cottage in Cotherstone, and the owner of large tracts of land locally, including chunks of Baldersdale. A widow in her eighties, disabled and wheelchair-bound by arthritis, caused in the main by many hunting accidents, she held an annual Harvest Home in her private chapel, followed by feasting and dancing in the ballroom, to which she invited estate workers and local luminaries. Hannah went too, and the cameras followed. Mrs Field's forthright manner, allied to a distinct sense of humour and a stentorian voice, made a deep impression on the director and his crew – and on the television critics of the major newspapers, to judge by the reviews published the day after the first of many transmissions of *Too Long a Winter*. She was virtually the only 'survivor', in publicity terms, of the remainder of the film's cast.

In her review in the *Guardian*, Nancy Banks-Smith even gave equal space to Mrs Field after her eulogy of Hannah:

'At the other end of the social see-saw was Mrs Field of Lartington Hall, widow of the grandson of millionaire Marshall Field. She is equally her own person. An exuberant hostess and a handful even in her eighties.

' "I think it's about time we were going to chapel, Madam", said her companion. "Oh, the hell", replied Mrs Field.'

In the *Morning Star*, a newspaper not given to writing about the rich and over-privileged, Stewart Lane wrote:

'The closing part of the programme was quite unforgettable, with the local lady of the manor, Mrs Field, combining Harvest Festival with America's Thanksgiving.

I didn't actually see anyone touch their forelock, but from the moment when Mrs Field accompanied the entry of the turkey with blasts of a hunting horn, to shots of Hannah primly seated, timidly moving one foot to the music, I knew this was a world far removed, not only in distance but in time, from the pace of urban life in which I move.'

Olive Julia Field has been accurately described as a well-loved eccentric. She was certainly a true daughter of a remarkably colourful family, for she was born a Saunderson, a line of famous

Mrs Field demonstrates her technique with the hunting horn during the filming of Too Long a Winter *in 1972* (Courtesy of Yorkshire Television)

Protestant fighters who were sent to settle in Ireland in the seventeeth century to quell the local rebels. They were given a large slice of counties Cavan and Fermanagh, including 20,000 acres from a grateful Cromwell after Robert Saunderson led troops to a famous victory at Drogheda. The Saundersons endured a rough passage when Catholic James II decreed that Protestants be persecuted in their turn, and Robert, the son of Cromwell's favourite, had to flee with a price on his head.

The family clung on, and Olive's father, Llewellyn, was one of three Saunderson brothers who cut a dash in nineteenth-century Dublin society as officers in the Eleventh Hussars. In 1863, he fell in love with one of the most beautiful women of the viceregal court, Lady Rachael Scott, daughter of the Earl of Clonmell. But the Earl vehemently opposed the match and would not even allow Llewellyn to enter his house.

The stricken suitor followed the tradition laid down in these matters and went to look for a fight. He volunteered to join the Regiment of Irish Light Horse, raised to go to the assistance of the Confederate forces in the American Civil War. By the time the two sides prepared to meet on the field of Gettysburg, Llewellyn had risen to be the aide-de-camp to General Robert E. Lee, the Confederate commander. Llewellyn created another Saunderson legend in the midst of that bloody battle. He was unhorsed, helpless and about to perish as a Federal trooper rode at him, sword raised. Llewellyn was a quick thinker, and gave the Masonic sign of distress on the faint chance that the trooper was also a member of the order. It worked. The trooper returned the salute with his sword and rode on by. General Lee lost the battle and surrendered, and so yet another Saunderson was on the run. But Llewellyn, as resourceful as his ancestors, gave his pursuers the slip and managed to find his way to the port of New Orleans where he boarded a ship bound for Ireland.

Llewellyn's exploits became the talk of Dublin and the hostility of the Earl of Clonmell melted. He gave his consent to the marriage and Llewellyn and Rachael lived for twenty years in Drunkeen, one of the Saunderson family homes. Olive was born there and might have stayed in Ireland for good but for the civil unrest created by the Irish demands for home rule at the time. In

1886, Llewellyn and his family were hissed and booed when they went to church. In dramatic Saunderson fashion, Llewellyn declared he was finished with Ireland and left to spend his later years travelling Europe, the young and lovely Olive in tow. They wintered in San Moritz.

Olive Saunderson and Norman Field met and fell in love in predictably romantic circumstances, when the Fields and the Saundersons were guests on board Lord Vestey's yacht on a cruise to Norway in 1909. They were married the same year in Dublin and returned to England to set up home.

The family Olive Saunderson married into had a story to equal her own, also stretching back to the seventeenth century when Zachariah Field left Yorkshire to settle in Massachusetts as a yeoman farmer. Norman Field's father was born there in 1831. His brother, Marshall Field, arrived three years later and went on to become a world legend as the Merchant Prince.

At the age of twenty-one, after some years as a clerk in a dry-goods store, Marshall went to Chicago, telling his sceptical boss that he would one day own a store so big that the doors alone would be worth more than the boss's entire business. It proved to be a conservative estimate. Marshall Field, who arrived in Chicago with one dollar in his pocket, built one of the world's greatest department stores and had enough spare energy to partner Pullman in the railcar business, become vice-president of both General Electric and the Edison Company, president of United States Steel, founder of the *Chicago Sun* and a bank which became one of the four biggest in the world. And he still found time to build up vast interests in meat packing and combine-harvesting giants. Gordon Selfridge, who went on to do rather well himself in the department-store business, started as one of Marshall's clerks. He was fired for impertinence. Marshall Field died in 1905 at the age of seventy-one. Five thousand of his employees attended the funeral. He left a personal fortune of $120 million, a staggering sum when the mathematical equation to bring it into line with its value today is calculated.

Norman's father, Marshall Field's elder brother, Joseph, did rather well himself in banking before accepting a job with Marshall. In 1879 he was sent to England to oversee the

Olive Field in her VAD uniform, 1914

Norman Field, Master of Lartington Hall

European side of the business, and settled in Cheshire within easy reach of the textile mills of Lancashire where he placed a lot of business. He had men in Paris, Berlin, Rome, Belfast and elsewhere to search out the merchandise needed to satisfy the voracious appetite of the Chicago store and, by 1875, was dispatching three-million-dollars' worth of goods each year across the Atlantic.

Norman was born in Altrincham, Cheshire, in 1880. He went to Eton where he began a lifelong interest in hunting by becoming Master of the Beagles. After completing his education he went to work in the family's Chicago businesses, but the call of the land, which ran strongly in his blood, proved too much. He went farming in Texas, but returned to England in 1908 and bought Morris Grange, with four farms, at Scotch Corner – a few miles from Lartington.

Severance from the family business did not reduce Norman's standard of living. In 1924, for instance, his income from the Field Family Trust in the United States, after all taxes were met, was £42,000. That, with what would certainly be substantial assets and income from other sources, combined with whatever part of the Saunderson fortune was brought into the marriage by Olive, allowed the Fields to indulge in a stylish and lavish way of life.

It was a permanent party, with a little gentlemanly farming on the side – interrupted, it must be said, by two World Wars when both laboured mightily for the common cause. From Morris Grange they hunted assiduously – their joint passion since they never had children of their own.

Norman became joint Master of the Zetland and, in 1924, took over the Westmeath Hounds in Eire. Every winter season he and Olive would entrain for the Saundersons' homeland, together with a selection of staff (said to number over sixty at one stage) and horses. Knockrin Castle was rented from Lord Boyne and the revelry was ceaseless.

On one of their visits, there was an uncanny, if hilarious, echo of the kind of political and religious turmoil experienced by Olive's family in years gone by. One day they were boarding a boat and noticed it contained a large number of sticks, shaped like rifles. On enquiring their purpose, the boatman explained they were used for drilling by the Orangemen on the estate, but they were passed on each week to the Sinn Feiners for their drill night!

Both Olive and Norman were skilled riders. Norman became a four-handicap polo player. He was devoted to sport, golfing around the world's best courses and still finding time to be an active member of the Royal Yacht Squadron. He owned a 70-ton yacht called *Revive*.

Olive's surplus energy was spent in working for the Red Cross Society and forming a Girl Guide and Scout troop. When Norman went to serve with the East Riding Yeomanry during the First World War, reaching the rank of captain, she worked from 7.00 a.m. to 5.00 p.m. as a VAD at the Red Cross Hospital in Richmond, travelling each day by pony and trap or bicycle, carrying a fresh egg from one of the Field farms. Soused herring was the standard hospital breakfast and she declared she couldn't stomach that at seven o'clock in the morning. Days off were spent riding to hounds. Grand though she was, she was rarely allowed to do any nursing, beyond changing the odd dressing. So she spent most of her time scrubbing floors. When war came again in 1939, she turned part of Lartington Hall into a convalescent hospital for war-wounded. The ballroom became a dormitory and two thousand servicemen passed through. Olive, acting as unpaid commandant with her customary zeal, was made a life member of the Red Cross, a signal honour. For his part, Norman handed over his yacht to the Royal Navy.

But when the nation was not at war the social round of the Fields was formidable. Olive, it is said, eventually grew tired of Morris Grange so, in 1919, Norman bought Lartington Hall with its 140 acres of parkland, 2 grouse moors, 2 lakes, 12 farms and most of the cottages in the village, and it became their principal residence for the rest of their lives. At the same time he also acquired the Streatlam Castle estate, childhood home of the Queen Mother, from the Earl of Strathmore. Consideration was given to living there, but the thought of sixty bedrooms and only one bathroom was too much. Legend has it that the place was once so deprived of modern conveniences that drinking water would sometimes be collected by a footman with a silver pitcher from a stream flowing in front of the main door, which originally served as a moat.

They gave Morris Grange, as a present, to the Red Cross as a home for sick children from the Teesdale area and considered how to improve Streatlam. The castle was in such a state of disrepair that they decided not to spend money on it, and eventually it was demolished. They chose instead to spend large sums of money on the farms, rebuilt the famous Orangery and installed a large indoor swimming pool in the courtyard. Norman also established a breeding stud of racehorses which produced many classic winners. A crowded board recalling the names of the stud's successful horses, along with several equestrian paintings, graced the reception area of Lartington Hall. They now reside on the walls of Rules of Covent Garden, said to be London's oldest restaurant, which is run by the son of Mrs Fields' nephew, John Mayhew.

Naturally, one of the first things the Fields did on arrival at Lartington Hall was to start their own pack of hounds. They went hunting most days of the season. The Hunt Balls are still recalled today with something akin to awe in the villages of Lartington and Cotherstone where several former servants of the Fields live in retirement. Mrs Betty Pearson, the lady who sold Belle Vue Cottage to Hannah, was one. She walked into Cotherstone at seven o'clock every morning to keep house for the 'Bothy Boys', the lads who looked after the hounds. Her husband, Jack, used to sell fruit and vegetables from a horse and cart, going as far as the top of Baldersdale to find custom. He was well known to all the elder members of the Hauxwell family, including Hannah's mother and father.

One particular family in Cotherstone must be able to claim the longest aggregate of service to the Fields, amounting to some hundreds of years. Mrs Dorothy Siswick was Olive Field's last personal maid. Her father was Head Groomsman at Streatlam, her mother the cook and her brother a footman. Her husband, Harry, was the head gardener to Lartington. Mrs Siswick first met Mrs Field when she was living with her parents at one of the estate cottages at Streatlam.

It was in 1924 when I was fourteen that I first went to work for Mrs Field. She came to visit Streatlam to look at the horses and

Mr and Mrs Siswick in 1990 (Courtesy of *Teesdale Mercury*)

I thought what a very handsome woman she was. She looked me over, said I seemed to be a nice girl and announced that she had just the job for me – taking her goats out for a walk! I was paid a few pence, and very welcome it was too.

When I was eighteen she gave me the job of housekeeper in the big cottage she kept at Streatlam to entertain her friends coming to swim in the pool and play tennis. They arrived from all over the place, from the big houses locally to as far away as London. They certainly knew how to enjoy themselves in those days. I would get a phone call to say they were coming, and sometimes I had to cook lunch for as many as sixty people. Occasionally, after a dance, they would decide to go swimming in the early hours of the morning, so all the cars would be lined up with their headlamps blazing to light up the pool.

Mrs Field was such a grand lady, and eventually I moved to Lartington to become her lady's maid. She could be abrupt at times but never held a grudge, and Mr Field was a real gentleman, always kind and polite. He broke his hip whilst hunting and the poor man walked with a limp from then on. Mrs Field rode to hounds twice a week, and I had to prepare and lay out her clothes before and after the hunt. Quite often she would return in such a mess, all covered in mud. She had one or two accidents in the field herself, and once broke her arm. In later years she suffered very badly from arthritis.

Mr and Mrs Field had separate bedrooms, which was the habit of the gentry. Every night the footman on duty had to place a bottle of the best champagne by the side of Mr Field's bed and it was invariably empty by the morning. The head of the staff was the butler, of course, a Mr Devenport. He was a disciplinarian, but a very fair and good man and organized quite a large number of servants, including three footmen and several housemaids and kitchen-workers. We had a head cook and three junior cooks to prepare the meals.

Mrs Field allowed her dogs to sleep in her bedroom. She had as many as six at one time, usually whippets and Pekinese, and one even gave birth to a litter in the bedroom. Once, when she was ill and I had to show the doctor in to see her, he was rather disconcerted to see the bedclothes on either side of Mrs Field appear to rise of their own accord – and four dogs emerged! I had to excuse myself and go out of the room, or I would have collapsed laughing at the doctor's reaction.

Yes, she really adored her dogs and there was a special graveyard for them in the grounds. One night all the other dogs set upon one poor whippet in her bathroom and virtually tore it to pieces. Mrs Field summoned the vet immediately, who said it was in a hopeless condition and should be put down at once. But she refused to allow that, and told him it had to live. It took forty-seven stitches to put that whippet back together but it lived.

Mr and Mrs Field also had separate cars. She always used a Rolls-Royce, and he a Bentley. They changed them a lot. And they always travelled separately, even when they were going to the same function. There were three chauffeurs on the staff and quite a few vehicles, including some Mercedes in later years.

Madam – I always called her that – used to go shopping in her Rolls-Royce to Barnard Castle. But she never got out. The car would pull up outside various shops and staff would come out to take her order.

Mr and Mrs Field had expensive tastes. They only liked the best. The finest wines were always delivered and the food had to match. But the grandest occasions were always the Hunt Balls. I would help Mrs Field dress. She had some lovely gowns sent from London, and plenty of jewellery and pearls, and a diamond watch from Cartier. She did look beautiful as she made her entrance down the main staircase. And the gentlemen were so handsome, too, in their Hunt livery. Lots of titled guests were always invited and once, in my mother's time as cook, Princess Mary came to dinner. Their Christmas parties were very special, too, and they always gave one for their staff the night after the one they threw for their friends.

Although they had no children of their own they did adopt a baby girl from the convalescent home for children at Morris Grange. She was called Mabel, and came from Middlesbrough. They sent her to London for elocution lessons and she grew into a lovely young lady. Sadly, she died of a brain haemorrhage in 1950 when she was scarcely in her twenties.

There was more sadness in 1957 when Mr Field died at the age of seventy-seven. There was a big funeral and my husband, the head gardener, made a cross of fifty roses for Mrs Field to place on his coffin. She was stricken and missed him terribly, but she wouldn't show it in public. The only time we saw any of his family from America was at the memorial service. Just one came, and he was so like Mr Field he must have been his brother.

The parties went on at Lartington Hall but it wasn't the same place after the death of Mr Field. Olive went on with her public service, working for the Red Cross, going regularly to Morris Grange, and becoming the longest-serving Alderman in England. All this was recognized by an MBE.

The number of servants at Lartington Hall dwindled, although Dorothy Siswick stayed with Olive until the end. Her other

Mrs Field with Horace

In earnest conversation with Hannah (Courtesy of Yorkshire
Television)

constant companion was a parrot named Horace. Olive steadfastly refused to move from the Hall, retreating gradually into the
east wing as the rest deteriorated. Birds nested in the
eighteenth-century ballroom but the chapel was carefully maintained and she also retained a butler and a chauffeur for the
Rolls-Royce.

Olive's spirit and capacity to command never diminished.
Apparently, she hugely enjoyed her part in the filming of *Too
Long a Winter* and liked the programme. When she saw Hannah
in the sequence where she played the tiny organ at Low Birk
Hatt, she tried to arrange for her to come to Lartington to try the
unique Aeolian pipe organ in the chapel. But, as Hannah recalls,
it was not to be.

No, regretfully Mrs Field died before it could be arranged. I
had only met her once before the film brought us together, but
I remember the occasion well. It was down the pasture near
Lartington on a day during the last war, when the weather
was very bad and I was going for the bus to Barnard Castle.
She was on foot going the other way, so I opened the gate for
her. 'It's awfully wild,' she said, 'but you are going the right
way' – she was proceeding east and going into the storm at the
time – and she thanked me for opening the gate.

Of course, everyone in the area knew Mrs Field – she even
owned two farms in Baldersdale, Foul Syke and Blackton. She
worked very hard for good causes and, during the war, in the
village and on the buses you often met servicemen in the light
blue uniform the wounded wore, who were recuperating at
Lartington Hall.

Hunting was a big part of her life, of course, and I have
mixed feelings about that subject. I'm well aware that foxes do
nasty things to lambs and poultry, and that sometimes there
are too many of them around. But maybe there are kinder
ways of keeping their numbers down.

Nobody thought anything about it during Mrs Field's
heyday. It was part of the way of life for the gentry, and not
the political issue it is today. A great social thing, too, and very
much part of the rural tradition. I have nothing against them

dressing up and riding around on horses but I don't like the thought of anything being hunted down, man or beast.

I have never seen a hunt in progress, although I recall vaguely as a child being taken to watch a Meet when I was visiting relatives in Piercebridge. I think it would have been the Zetland, and – who knows – Mrs Field may have been riding with them that day.

Nor, I must confess, have I ever seen a fox. Well, not a live one, anyway. Sam Fawcett used to keep a stuffed one in a glass case, which is the nearest I have ever been to one.

Less than six months after the transmission of *Too Long a Winter*, when her personality came through strongly enough to excite much public response, Olive Field was dead.

One of the sequences of the film featured Mrs Field being driven in her Rolls-Royce by her elderly chauffeur, Arthur Shields. On 20 June 1973, he was driving her, together with a friend, towards Morris Grange when their car collided head-on with a lorry. All three were killed.

This was a sudden and tragic end to a spectacular life. Olive was eighty-seven.

Nearly two decades after her death, they still talk about Olive Field in Teesdale. She has a permanent place in local folklore, and one story regularly told recalls the occasion when she and her retinue arrived at Darlington Station to catch the train to London. They were late – apparently, Mrs Field was invariably late – and as they approached the platform the train began to leave, whereupon Mrs Field set off in pursuit, bellowing 'Stop that bloody train!', in a voice richly laden with authority.

The message somehow got through to someone with the ability to obey her command – possibly the engine-driver, who may have thought it was an order direct from heaven – and the train ground to a halt. In front of a stunned and amazed assembly of railwaymen and passengers, Mrs Field boarded with a flourish and signalled her consent for the train to recommence its journey. Trains, taxis . . . they were all the same to Olive Field.

She was one of the last survivors of a lifestyle which is now extinct and despite the faint echoes of feudalism, its demise has made the world a less colourful place.

14

Ambition, Music, Politics...and the Future

H annah Hauxwell is essentially a very private person. Her upbringing instilled in her certain strict ground rules, chief among which is modesty. Together these two factors have tended to cloak her personality, leaving an impression of excessive timidity. Those who know her well also know that this is inaccurate. She has strong opinions on several subjects, including politics, but not all for public consumption.

And she has nursed ambitions.

Hannah is obviously a natural musician, although the aforementioned modesty forbids her to agree with that assessment. But as a child she quickly learned to play both piano and organ with none of the pain and stress often endured by most youngsters, even those with natural skills. More than once she has been asked, without prior warning, to sit down there and then and play an instrument – usually for a film sequence – and she always complies without a flicker of nerves. She has often stated that, for her, music is one of life's most important elements.

It is a great pity that Fate placed her in a situation which allowed her no chance to properly exploit an undeniable talent.

If I could have asked for a gift, I suppose it would have been the ability to make a living as a musician. It must be marvellous to be an instrumentalist or a singer good enough to hold an audience in your spell, like Maria Callas or Yehudi Menuhin. But I would have had to be at the top, not just scraping along. And I would have wanted to be an instrumentalist, not a singer. Either the piano or the organ would have been my choice although, to play at concerts, I suppose the piano would have been the preference.

I have some sheet music which belonged to my mother, unless the mice and rats at Low Birk Hatt have chewed it to bits. But I can only play by ear these days. I could read music at one time but not now. Mother could play both by ear and by reading. But I have a theory that if you have two musicians, both trained and able to play anything that is put before them, but only one of them has the ability to play by ear as well, then he or she will be able to project more life, beauty and expression than the other. My late cousin, Norman, who was a very talented musician, shared the same opinion.

As far as my own taste in music is concerned I like everything from ragtime to opera, but prefer the classical composers such as Mozart, Beethoven, Strauss and Tchaikovsky. I'm old-fashioned when it comes to musicals, usually drawing the line after Sigmund Romberg. I'm not that keen on the modern composers, like Andrew Lloyd Webber. I wouldn't go out of my way to hear their music.

Not that I have had much opportunity to appreciate live music. I did once have the pleasure of going with Norman to hear Reginald Forte do a recital on the organ at Middleton in Teesdale Chapel, which is closed now. I do like a good organist, particularly when a traditional organ is used. I know they make some remarkable instruments now, electronic ones, I believe, which can produce all kinds of sounds, be it piano or clarinet or anything. And the people who can play them are very clever indeed. But that's not the kind of music I like.

I prefer the traditional organ, and I found out that Tony Benn also holds this view. We were appearing together at a literary lunch in Cleethorpes – he was promoting the latest edition of his diaries – and someone was playing the organ whilst we were eating. I heard him mention something about organs to another guest so I put my oar in and started such a nice conversation. It turned out that he shared my liking for the more conventional kind of organ.

Mr Benn is a thoroughly charming man, and I was pleased to pay tribute to him when I got up to speak. I like him for being a rebel, and we agree on several issues, although I am not sure I would go along with some of his proposals to abolish the monarchy and the House of Lords. But he has a good Christian upbringing and outlook.

Hannah with the 'rebel' she admires. A conversation with Tony Benn at a literary lunch. (Courtesy of Grimsby Evening Telegraph)

Now I know it's traditional for Daleswomen not to have an interest in politics, but our family was Liberal by and large. Uncle certainly was, and Great-Uncle John Tallentire was a great admirer of Lloyd George. I have used my vote in the General Election once or twice, but not recently.

Personally, I am against extremists of any political persuasion. I could point to quite a few leaders about whom I am not enthusiastic but I will refrain from naming them, and concentrate on those I like.

David Steel is one of them. Indeed, I recall one occasion when I heard him and Tony Benn separately on the radio and they were expressing essentially the same opinions about the same issues. I would have liked to have seen David Steel at

316

Number 10. I well remember him as one of the voices in the wilderness during the Falklands affair. Not many spoke out against sending the Taskforce – and I also admired him for taking over the Liberal Party in very difficult circumstances. I like several of his ideals, including, perhaps, the campaign for proportional representation. The present system does seem unfair.

Denis Healey is another politician I admire, and I tend to agree with the view that he is the best leader the Labour Party never had. He, too, has the courage to speak out, and so has Ted Heath, whether what they say is right or wrong or agrees with the party line. I like honesty but that is not possible if you are obliged to obey the party whip. I suppose a lot of people of different parties have similar ideals, good and decent Members of Parliament who all want the right things, such as the proper maintenance of the Health Service and provision of houses for the homeless. But they are not in a position to do anything about it unless they obey their conscience instead of the whip.

Power, or the prospect of power, is a very heady thing and some people cannot seem to cope with it. That's probably why there are so many different parties, why the Social Democratic Party and the Liberal Party split. I wonder if that is why we are stuck with the present regime – because there isn't a single, united opposition.

Personally, I would like to see a future government formed from all the parties as a coalition. Then they could all pool their energy and intelligence into solving all the problems we face.

As for my own personal future . . . well, I have my own Five Year Plan to sort out the confusion in which I live. But I think I may have to extend it – just like the politicians – because I haven't achieved anything in all the time I have been in my new home. I know there are a lot of boxes piled around the place. Some contain things which are valuable and useful and others, I have to admit, have stuff which I really ought to throw away. It won't be easy because of my hoarding instinct, but I shall really have to try. Yes, sorting out the house must be a major priority for the future, or else I will get into a real pickle again, like I did at Low Birk Hatt.

I do wish I could find more energy to get on with it. I'm afraid I suffer continually from tiredness, but the job will have to be done.

Looking ahead, I suppose travel would be nice, if only the opportunity arose and I had the courage to go with it. I have a wish to go to Paris. It would be lovely to walk along the Champs-Elysées and see the Arc de Triomphe, go into the Louvre to look at the Mona Lisa, and visit the Opera House. I have heard of a café near the Opera, where, if you sit long enough, they say you can see the whole world go by. That's the story they tell anyway. There are lots of other places I would like to visit – Vienna, for the music, would be high on my list – but I don't know how I would get there. By the shortest sea route probably, because the prospect of flying in an aeroplane rather daunts me.

But I have nothing at all to complain about. If I hadn't been 'discovered', as I suppose I must describe it, then I would have been on the same old path, up at Low Birk Hatt and miserable.

I know they say I am a celebrity, but I take it all with a pinch of salt. Fame is a very fickle mistress. I will enjoy it while it lasts.

I have a lot going for me. I have good friends, and if I can keep my faculties – if my eyesight behaves itself and my hearing stays good – then I shall be content.

Acknowledgements

Part One: Seasons of My Life was largely based on taped conversations with Hannah Hauxwell, principally conducted by Kathy Rooney, to whom Hannah and Barry Cockcroft express profound gratitude. Barry Cockcroft also extends thanks to former residents of Baldersdale who so generously assisted with their recollections and photographs of the past, particularly John and Marie Thwaites, the Fawcett family and Lavinia Thwaites.

For *Part Two: Daughter of the Dales* Hannah Hauxwell and Barry Cockcroft extend their gratitude for unstinting assistance and support to John and Marie Thwaites, Mike Prosser, the Fawcett family, Margaret Nixon, Kelvin Walker, Lavinia Thwaites, Elsie Birdsall, Harold L. Beadle, Dr Philip Gates, Betty Pearson, Dorothy and Harry Siswick, Arthur Newlove, Derek Mayhew, Eric Stainthorpe, the new owners of Low Birk Hatt, Mary Hamilton, Betty Wall, Jim McTaggart of the *Teesdale Mercury*, Margaret Higginson, Sarah Wallace, Valerie Buckingham, Carol Hainstock, Barbara Bagnall, Brian Jeeves, Kathy Rooney, and Vivien Green.

319

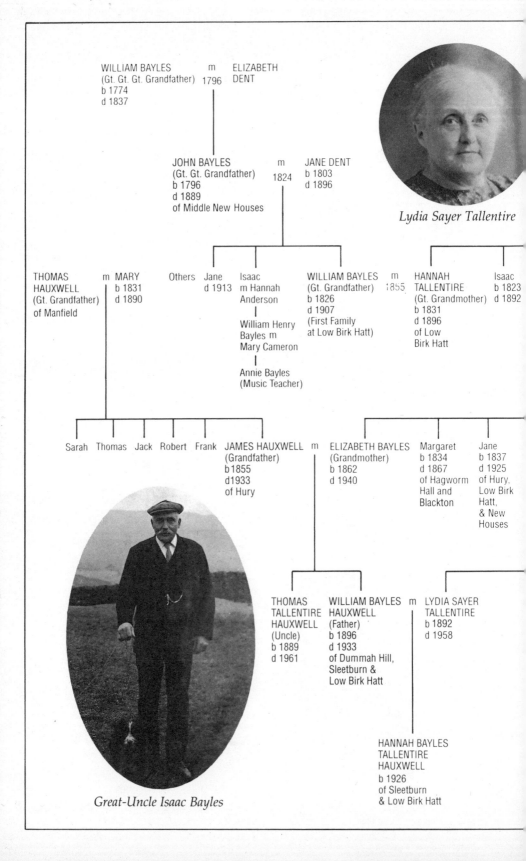

WILLIAM BAYLES   m   ELIZABETH
(Gt. Gt. Gt. Grandfather) 1796 DENT
b 1774
d 1837

JOHN BAYLES   m   JANE DENT
(Gt. Gt. Grandfather) 1824 b 1803
b 1796   d 1896
d 1889
of Middle New Houses

Lydia Sayer Tallentire

THOMAS   m MARY   Others Jane   Isaac   WILLIAM BAYLES   m   HANNAH   Isaac
HAUXWELL   b 1831   d 1913 m Hannah   (Gt. Grandfather) 1855 TALLENTIRE   b 1823
(Gt. Grandfather) d 1890   Anderson   b 1826   (Gt. Grandmother) d 1892
of Manfield   d 1907   b 1831
                         William Henry (First Family   d 1896
                         Bayles m   at Low Birk Hatt)   of Low
                         Mary Cameron   Birk Hatt

Annie Bayles
(Music Teacher)

Sarah Thomas Jack Robert Frank   JAMES HAUXWELL   m   ELIZABETH BAYLES   Margaret   Jane
                              (Grandfather)   (Grandmother)   b 1834   b 1837
                              b1855   b 1862   d 1867   d 1925
                              d1933   d 1940   of Hagworm of Hury,
                              of Hury   Hall and   Low Birk
                                                     Blackton   Hatt,
                                                                       & New
                                                      Houses

THOMAS   WILLIAM BAYLES   m   LYDIA SAYER
TALLENTIRE   HAUXWELL   TALLENTIRE
HAUXWELL   (Father)   b 1892
(Uncle)   b 1896   d 1958
b 1889   d 1933
d 1961   of Dummah Hill,
             Sleetburn &
             Low Birk Hatt

HANNAH BAYLES
TALLENTIRE
HAUXWELL
b 1926
of Sleetburn
& Low Birk Hatt

Great-Uncle Isaac Bayles